BestMasters

Springer awards „BestMasters“ to the best master's theses which have been completed at renowned universities in Germany, Austria, and Switzerland.
The studies received highest marks and were recommended for publication by supervisors. They address current issues from various fields of research in natural sciences, psychology, technology, and economics.
The series addresses practitioners as well as scientists and, in particular, offers guidance for early stage researchers.

Simon Weiler

Dynamics of Cross-Border Flow-Performance Relationships

The Case of European Equity (UCITS) Funds

Springer Gabler

Simon Weiler
Wien, Austria

Master´s Thesis, University of Applied Sciences (BFI) Vienna 2014

BestMasters
ISBN 978-3-658-08153-9 ISBN 978-3-658-08154-6 (eBook)
DOI 10.1007/978-3-658-08154-6

Library of Congress Control Number: 2014956552

Springer Gabler

Printed on acid-free paper

Springer Gabler is a brand of Springer Fachmedien Wiesbaden
Springer Fachmedien Wiesbaden is part of Springer Science+Business Media
(www.springer.com)

Table of contents

List of tables IX

List of illustrations XI

List of appendices XIII

Abbreviations XV

Abstract XVII

1. Introduction 1
    1.1. Problem outline and significance 1
    1.2. Review of comparable and related research 3
    1.3. Research questions and hypotheses 6
    1.4. Set up & structure 9
    1.5. Primary sources 12
2. Properties of the mutual fund industry 14
    2.1. Properties of mutual funds 14
        2.1.1. Purpose and benefits of mutual funds 14
        2.1.2. Active versus passive mutual funds 15
        2.1.3. Open-ended versus closed-end funds 16
        2.1.4. Justification for existence 17
    2.2. Market development and competition 18
        2.2.1. Market size and development: Global 18
        2.2.2. Market size and development: Europe 20
        2.2.3. Competition within the European fund industry 24
    2.3. Economies of scale 28
    2.4. Boutique versus large fund management companies 29
3. Outperformance & performance persistence 32
    3.1. How to identify outperformers 32

3.1.1. Asset class classifications 32
3.1.2. Performance evaluation 33
3.2. Persistence of mutual fund returns 37
3.3. Life-cycle theory 39
4. Investor behavior 42
4.1. Behavioral finance and the flow-performance relationship 42
4.2. Incorporating investor irrationalities in quantitative models 44
5. Methodology & definitions 45
5.1. Empirical set up 45
5.1.1. Data source 45
5.1.2. Data horizon and frequency 46
5.1.3. Data focus & sample limitations 47
5.1.4. Required data types 50
5.2. Data sample 53
5.3. Quantitative methods 56
5.3.1. General remarks 56
5.3.2. Correlation models 58
5.3.3. Regression models 60
6. Time series analysis 64
6.1. Correlation analysis 64
6.2. Bivariate linear regression analysis 70
6.3. Multivariate linear regression analysis 75
7. Empiric evidence 79
7.1. Research question & hypothesis 1 79
7.1.1. Research question & hypothesis 1.1 79
7.1.2. Research question & hypothesis 1.2 80

7.2. Research question & hypothesis 2 81

7.3. Research question & hypothesis 3 81

Conclusion 83

Bibliography 85

List of tables

Table 1: Summary statistics for mutual funds with European sales registration ... 25
Table 2: Summary statistics for European fund management companies 26
Table 3: Market share of Lipper Global asset classes 27
Table 4: Market share of Top-10 sub-asset classes (only taking into account primary tranches) 28
Table 5: Correlation-test details: percentage growth vs. lagged fund (net) flows.. 66
Table 6: Correlation-test details: Volatility vs. lagged fund (net) flows 68
Table 7: Correlation-test details: Sharpe ratio vs. lagged fund (net) flows 70
Table 8: Combined results of pooled bivariate OLS-regressions 71
Table 9: Coefficients of bivariate OLS-regression: flow~percentage growth 72
Table 10: Coefficients of bivariate OLS-regression: flow~volatility 73
Table 11: Coefficients of bivariate OLS-regression: flow~Sharpe ratio................ 74
Table 12: Results of multivariate OLS-regression models measuring convexity .. 75
Table 13: Results of extended multivariate OLS-regression models 76
Table 14: Results of extended multivariate OLS-regression model measuring total AUM impact.. 77

List of illustrations

Illustration 1: Market size development: Global mutual fund industry (2000 – Q1 2013) ... 18
Illustration 2: Market size development: European mutual fund industry (2000 – Q1 2013) ... 20
Illustration 3: Industry growth comparison: Europe versus Global (ex. Europe) ... 21
Illustration 4: Cumulative market share distribution of European domiciles (Q1 2013). ... 22
Illustration 5: European mutual fund market: historical Gini coefficients (2006-Q1 2013) ... 23
Illustration 6: Relative growth of European tax havens as favored fund domicile (2000-Q1 2013) ... 24
Illustration 7: Lorenz curve: Volume distribution of European mutual fund companies ... 26
Illustration 8: Calculation of percentage growth ... 34
Illustration 9: Calculation of monthly volatility ... 34
Illustration 10: Calculation of Sharpe ratio ... 35
Illustration 11: Simplified demonstration of employed time-lag methodology ... 46
Illustration 12: Methodology of Lipper fund flow module ... 51
Illustration 13: Development of the number of incorporated sample size over time ... 53
Illustration 14: Comparison: Number of fund liquidations vs. new funds over time ... 54
Illustration 15: Development of average relative fund (net) flow observations over time (annual figures, monthly rolling) ... 55
Illustration 16: Development of observed fund volumes over time ... 56
Illustration 17: Formula for normalization of variables ... 58
Illustration 18: Calculation of Spearman's ρ (in case of no ties) ... 58
Illustration 19: Calculation of Spearman's ρ (in case of ties) ... 59
Illustration 20: Calculating t-values for hypothesis testing ... 60
Illustration 21: Bivariate-OLS regression model: Flow-Percentage growth relationship ... 61
Illustration 22: Bivariate-OLS regression model: Flow-Volatility relationship ... 61
Illustration 23: Bivariate-OLS regression model: Flow-Sharpe ratio relationship .. 61
Illustration 24: Piecewise bivariate-OLS regression mode ... 61
Illustration 25: Multivariate OLS-regression model measuring convexity ... 62
Illustration 26: Extended multivariate OLS-regression model ... 63
Illustration 27: Extended multivariate OLS-regression model measuring total AUM impact ... 63
Illustration 28: Monthly rolling rank-correlation: percentage growth vs. lagged fund (net) flows ... 65

Illustration 29: Monthly rolling rank-correlation: volatility vs. lagged fund (net) flows 67
Illustration 30: Monthly rolling rank-correlation: Sharpe ratio vs. lagged fund (net) flows 69
Illustration 31: Connected slopes of piecewise flow~percentage growth regression 73
Illustration 32: Connected slopes of piecewise flow~volatility regression 74
Illustration 33: Connected slopes of piecewise flow~Sharpe ratio regression 75

List of appendices

Appendix A: correlation-test details: flow~percentage growth 91
Appendix B: correlation-test details: flow~volatility 92
Appendix C: correlation-test details: flow~Sharpe ratio 93
Appendix D: geographical database coverage: Lipper for Investment Management 94

Abbreviations

AUD	Australian Dollar
AUM	Assets under Management
BVI	Bundesverband Investment und Asset Management e.V.
CAIA	Chartered Alternative Investment Analyst
D.C.	District of Columbia
ed.	edition
EFAMA	European Fund and Asset Management Association
e.g.	exempli gratia
EHM	Efficient Market Hypothesis
et al.	et alli (masculine), et aliae (feminine) or et alia (neuter)
ETF	Exchange-Traded Fund
EUR	Euro
EURm	Million Euro
GBM	Geometric Brownian Motion
GmbH	Gesellschaft mit beschränkter Haftung
HSBC	Hong Kong and Shanghai Banking Corporation
ICI	Investment Company Institute
i.e.	id est
IPO	Initial Public Offering
LIM	Lipper for Investment Management
NAV	Net Asset Value
n.p.	no place of publication given.
OLS	Ordinary Least Squares
p.	page
pp.	pages
Q	quarter
ρ	Spearman's rank correlation coefficient (rho)
SEC	Securities and Exchange Commision
S&P	Standard & Poor's
THB	Thailand Baht
UK	United Kingdom
US	United States
VaR	Value at Risk

Abstract

Trotz des weitverbreiteten rechtlichen Hinweises „Vergangenheitsperformance ist keine Garantie für zukünftige Erträge“ ist es unbestreitbar, dass sich Investoren bei der Auswahl von Investmentfonds dennoch in beachtlichem Ausmaß von vergangenheitsbezogenen Performance-Werten (mangels adäquater Alternativen) leiten lassen. Die hier zugrunde liegenden „Performance-Zufluss“ Beziehungen wurden bereits ausführlich von einer Vielzahl wissenschaftlicher Projekte untersucht. Hierbei konnte generell ein signifikant positiver und konvexer Zusammenhang zwischen Vergangenheitsperformance und darauffolgenden Nettomittelzuflüssen festgestellt werden. Bislang fokussierten sich solche Arbeiten bei ihren Analysen jedoch ausschließlich auf Fonds eines ganz bestimmten Domizils (insbesondere USA). Aus diesem Grund widmet sich die hier vorliegende Arbeit einem gänzlich neuen Sample, welches unter der Hypothese abgeleitet wurde, dass Investoren einer homogenen und transparenten Investmentregion (Europa) - zum öffentlichen Vertrieb zugelassene Fonds - unabhängig ihres Domizils auswählen.

Auf Basis umfangreicher statistischer Tests (monatlich rollierender Rang-Korrelationen, (stückweiser) bivariater sowie multivariater linearer Regressionen) findet diese Arbeit umfangreiche empirische Beweise dafür, dass die wichtigsten Erkenntnisse vergleichbarer Studien – ein signifikanter positiver sowie tendenziell konvexer Zusammenhang zwischen Vergangenheitsperformance und zukünftigen Nettomittelzuflüssen - auch für ein überregionales Sample von Europa Aktienfonds mit UCITS-Struktur zutreffend sind. Gerade für den, von zunehmend grenzüberschreitenden Fondstransaktionen (etwa aufgrund des Vormarsches der UCITS-Hubs Luxemburg und Irland) geprägten, europäischen Fondsmarkt liefert diese Arbeit wichtige Einblicke in die überregionale Absatz-Dynamik von Europa Aktienfonds. Zukünftige Studien könnten sich der entwickelten Methodologie bedienen und das Sample auf weitere relevante Assetklassen – bis hin zum gesamten in Europa verfügbaren Fondsuniversum – ausdehnen.

1. Introduction

1.1. Problem outline and significance

When reading any arbitrarily chosen mutual fund fact sheet the legally required standard disclaimer stating "past performance is not indicative of future results" [1] usually cannot be overlooked. However, even though past performance or past data in general might not be a good indicator of future results, what factors other than past performance should investors focus on, when making their investment decisions? Future results, if anything can only be simulated by using complex mathematical models, which still make broad use of past track records (e.g. via a geometric Brownian motion model[2]).

Therefore, and as a result of the absence of appropriate alternatives, (retail) investors often have no other choice than letting their investment decisions be extensively influenced by past performance or at least past data of any kind (e.g. risk-parameters). But it is not just the investors who let themselves be largely steered by past data. Also other major stake-holders of the global mutual fund industry are affected by this phenomenon:

First of all fund management companies (respectively asset management companies) frequently tend to use selected past performance figures and risk-parameters (which are based on past data also[3]) as a foundation of advertising campaigns and unique selling propositions.[4]

Secondly financial media as well as main-stream media regularly publish mutual fund rankings that are mostly designed in a rather straight-forward, if not to say unidirectional way. They are usually generated at the end of a calendar year and frequently focus on just one rather isolated performance figure (e.g. 5-year annual compound return or 5-year annualized Sharpe ratio).[5]

---

[1] SEC (2010) online.

[2] Brandimarte (2003) p. 316.

[3] E.g. Sharpe- or Sortino-ratio.

[4] SEC (2007) online.

[5] E.g. Baird's Advisory Services Research (2011) pp. 3-4. or HSBC (2005) p. 52.

Additionally the majority of more or less independently provided mutual fund ratings, such as the well-established "Morningstar-Ratings" or "Lipper-Leaders" are solely based on past performance.[6]

The just described phenomena further underscore the pretended importance and prominence of past performance as they in a certain sense can create a vicious circle (or chain):

(i) As a result of a certain past performance (no matter whether based on skill or luck) a mutual fund is being considered as an "outperformer" by a fund rating agency or a media ranking.[7]

(ii) Since both, ratings as well as rankings, are publicly available to investors, they can for the first time be directly or indirectly "steered" by the respective results.[8]

(iii) In a third step the fund management companies (providing the "outperformers") can actively and publicly advertise their latest rating/ranking achievements to investors.[9]

(iv) Media puts further emphasis on recently designated "outperformers" by publishing special reports/interviews with the respective fund management team.[10]

Even though a variety of studies has already proven past (out-) performance of mutual funds tends not to be persistent, empirical research depicts that investors generally disregard this fact in their investment decisions by applying and interpreting past performance figures in a prospective way. Thus outperforming mutual funds should naturally have an edge over worse performing funds (in terms of generating new fund inflows), as they appear to investors more attractively.[11]

---

[6] Hereil et al. (2010) p. 2.

[7] Hereil et al. (2010) p. 2.

[8] Jones (2009) p. 73.

[9] SEC (n.a.) p. 21.

[10] Ciccotello (2009) pp. 17-18.

[11] Hereil et al. (2010) pp. 2-5.

1.2. Review of comparable and related research

Fund management companies are mainly financing themselves through the annual management fee which defines itself as a percentage of assets under management (AUM).[12] Thus asset management companies as well as their respective fund managers should have a natural and economically justified interest into which (endogenous and exogenous) factors are actually driving fund in- or outflows. Hence it is not entirely surprising that there is already a variety of research available which focused on some aspects of such relationships and the fund flow-past performance figure in particular. However, also not completely astonishing[13], most of those research publications have so far focused on the case for the US mutual fund market.[14]

Most foundational work within this particular research field has been carried out by Ippolito (1992) and Sirri/Tufano (1993), both examining the flow-performance relationship for US-domiciled equity mutual funds by applying piecewise linear regression models. Based on their researched empirical sample they could identify that (i) lagged fund flows are significantly related to a fund's past performance and (ii) the fund flow- past performance relationship is depicting a convex nature, thereby indicating that mutual fund investors are buying past-winners at a higher rate than they are selling past-losers.[15]

Chevalier/Ellison (1997) extended the research on the flow-performance relationship by focusing on potentially occurring agency conflicts between mutual fund management companies and their investors (with mutual fund management companies generally aiming to maximize inflows and mutual fund investors seeking to be provided with a maximum of (risk-adjusted) excess return). They conclude that, based on a convex flow-performance relationship (which by its nature, is rewarding winners stronger than it is punishing losers), mutual fund managers are incen-

---

[12] SEC (2013) online.

[13] As chapter 2.2.1. will disclose in more detail, almost half of the global mutual fund volume can be attributed to the US domicile as per end of Q1 2013.

[14] E.g. Ferreira et al. (2012) p. 1759. or Ber et al. (2007) p. 2.

[15] Ferreira et al. (2012) p. 1759.

tivized to either increase or decrease their (year-to-date) risk profile for the sake of benefitting from maximized next year inflows.[16]

More recently, Ber et al. (2007) have contributed to the mutual fund (net) flow-performance research field by empirically examining the flow-performance relation for Germany-domiciled equity mutual funds. In line with the findings of US-focused research works, they also indentified the flow-performance relationship for German equity funds to be of a convex nature (although less pronounced than as compared to the findings of the US-research).[17] Additionally Ber et al. (2007) have researched the influence of fund family characteristics as explanatory variables within flow-performance regressions. They detected that both (i) (lagged) fund family size as well as (ii) concurrently observed (net) flows into the fund family[18] have a statistically significant and positive impact on a respective single fund's flows. Moreover they found out that an increasing number of funds, a fund family comprises, is demonstrating a statistically negative influence on a single fund's lagged (net) flows, if (and only if) the other fund family constituents can be attributed to the same segment (asset class).[19] Ber et al. (2007) refer to this key-finding as "cannibalism effects".[20]

Ferreira et al. (2012) are known to be the first authors who are seeking to test the geographical consistency of the (convex) flow-performance relationship by both individually as well as aggregately (pooled across countries) examining equity mutual fund samples of 28 different countries around the world.[21] In line with previous research (e.g. Ippolito (1992) and Sirri/Tufano (1993)) they also seek to account for a potentially convex (or otherwise non-linear) relation by setting up piecewise linear regressions.[22] Ferreira et al. (2012) conclude that a statistically significant convex flow-performance is also identifiable for a globally aggregated sample of

---

[16] Chevalier/Ellison (1997) p. 1167.

[17] Ber et al. (2007) pp. 18-19.

[18] By "fund family" Ber et al. (2007) are referring to the total product portfolio of a fund management company.

[19] Ber et al. (2007) pp. 33.

[20] Ber et al, (2007) pp. 22.

[21] Ferreira et al. (2012) p. 1759.

[22] Ferreira et al. (2012) p. 1765.

equity mutual funds.[23] Having said that, flow-performance relationships (as well as their potentially non-linear features) are far away from being universally valid across all countries. Based on the broad set of individual country assessments that are being presented within Ferreira et al. (2012), it is clearly observable that the prevailing and foundational findings of US-focused research (e.g. Ippolito (1992), Sirri/Tufano (1993) or Chevalier/Ellison (1997)) are not directly applicable to other countries – amongst their data sample only 10 out of 28 researched countries are depicting a statistically significant convexity within their flow-performance relationship.[24]

Based on the just presented review of previous research publications that can be attributed to the scope of this thesis (i.e. aspects of the flow-performance relationship for mutual funds) it can now be summarized that

(i) all the above stated studies have been able to detect a significant positive relation between past performance and lagged (net) fund flows and that the flow-performance relationship can generally be assessed as depicting a significant asymmetric (convex) nature (with the exception of Ferreira et al. (2012) who demonstrated that significant convex flow-performance relationships are not observable for all countries globally).

(ii) the prevailing ideas of the flow-performance relationship (with all its features) are generally referring to the foundational (pioneer) research works of Ippolito (1992), Sirri/Tufano (1993) and Chevalier/Ellison (1997), who all were focusing on (a) the US-mutual fund market and (b) equity mutual funds, and thus contain some bias. Ber et al. (2007) and Ferreira et al. (2012) have proven that US-findings are not universally valid for (geographically) different samples.

In respect of the detailed methodology and focus, the above mentioned research publications have chosen, the majority of works have decided to limit their fund sample based on a specific fund domicile (e.g. US fund domicile in the case of Ippolito (1992), Sirri/Tufano (1993) and Chevalier/Ellison (1997) or German fund domicile in the case of Ber et al. (2007)). Although Ferreira et al. (2012) did perform a pooled flow-performance regression about a larger sample of observed

[23] Ferreira et al. (2012) p. 1767.

[24] Ferreira et al. (2012) p. 1769.

countries (28 different fund domiciles), they still also assessed a fund's relative performance (by means of rank attribution) on a fund domicile level.[25] Thus all the so far employed methodologies are somehow assuming that only mutual funds of one and the same fund domicile are competing against each other. While such a perception of mutual fund competition might be valid for the US-mutual fund market (e.g. due to geographical or mutual market penetration-wise exceptional position), it is (highly) questionable for the European market, where investors typically have the possibility to choose funds from a wide range of fund domiciles.[26] In order to also account for such conditions of competition this thesis will employ different, innovative[27] methodology approaches for modeling some aspects of the flow-performance relationship. Details on the herewith associated explicit research questions and hypothesis are provided in the subsequent sub-chapter 1.3..

1.3. Research questions and hypotheses

As chapter 1.2. has just outlined, a multitude of previous studies and research papers has already examined mutual fund investor behaviour (by means of observing the relation between past performance and (lagged) past net fund flows) and detected that, regardless of a generally identifiable non-persistent return property, a tendency towards investment decisions based on past performance figures is observable.[28] To be more specific this "causal tendency" is primarily based upon the fact that the majority of previous research works have found the underlying flow-performance relationship to be of (statistically) significant convex nature.

The methodologies of all of the reviewed comparable previous research works (to be found in chapter 1.2.) have been assuming that, when seeking to conduct an investment, mutual fund investors are solely comparing funds that belong to the exact same fund domicile. Since this assumption could be questioned for more opened mutual fund markets (and Europe in particular), this thesis is aiming to firstly research aspects of the flow-performance relationship by making use of an

---

[25] Ferreira et al. (2012) p. 1765.

[26] See chapter 2.2. for details on (geographical) market specifics and market developments.

[27] Within this particular research field.

[28] Hereil et al. (2010) pp. 2-5.

alternative perception of competition that is suggesting that investors are comparing funds of all types of domiciles (as long as they have a legal access[29]).

Based on these principal assumptions the following research question, sub-research questions as well as hypothesis have been deduced:

Research question 1

Which results and implications does an extensive set of flow-performance relationship analyses deliver when being applied to a new cross-country data sample that has been selected based on a - so far – unconventional competition assumption?

Hypothesis 1

The employed alternative perception of competition is – a priori – only impacting the research in the sense of causing the incorporation of comparably larger fund sample.[30] Thus the author is not expecting the general findings and implications of previous research works to be significantly hurt when being applied to this new sample (and methodology). Hence a statistically significant convex flow-performance relationship is also anticipated for this research sample. The herewith associated sub-research questions and hypotheses are as follows:

- **Research question 1.1**

  Based on the researched (empirical) mutual fund sample: Is there a statistically significant (positive) correlation between mutual fund performance (with the term "performance" covering the following three different types of performance- respective risk-figures: (i) percentage growth, (ii) volatility, (iii) Sharpe ratio)[31] and lagged mutual fund (net) inflows detectable?

- **Hypothesis 1.1**

  Based on the generally homogenous findings of previous research, also this thesis is expecting to be able to reject the null hypothesis for all three researched flow-performance relationships.

---

[29] I.e. the fund is registered for distribution within the investor's market.

[30] As the research is no longer limited to just one fund domicile.

[31] Details on the researched performance- and risk-figures are provided in chapter 3.1.2.

- **Research question 1.2**

  Are the researched flow-performance relationships depicting a linear or non-linear connection? In case of detected non-linear relations: are they formed in a convex or concave way?

- **Hypothesis 1.2**

  Also in respect to the exact form of the researched relationships, this thesis is expecting results not to differ dramatically from previous publications and thus non-linear (convex) relationships are anticipated for this new sample as well.

The tasks necessary for answering the first request question (and its sub-research questions and hypotheses) more or less only constitute the application of already existing models to a new data sample which has been derived by employing a – so far – unconventional methodology. Since this alone would not sufficiently meet the author's desire of adding entirely new contributions to the flow-performance relationship research, this thesis will also be examining its sample along the following, additional research questions:

Research question 2

Comparable research has generally been examining flow-performance relationships by conducting pooled regressions over the whole observation period and hence could not detect whether coefficients have been subject to certain (time-specific) trends. Thus also the subsequent research question has been derived: How are (selected) flow-performance relationship coefficients behaving over time? Are there any indications for trend-like developments of coefficient values?

Hypothesis 2

Since the quantitative empirical models of this thesis will process data of a substantial observation period (covering major disruptive events such as the emergence of the sub-prime mortgage crisis, the global financial crisis starting 2008 or the Eurozone crisis), the observation of a certain kind of trend-like development within coefficient values (e.g. increased investor focus on risk- or risk-adjusted performance figures after the outbreak of the 2008 financial crisis) is assumed to be legitimate.

Research question 3

With the exception of Ber et al. (2007)[32] the methodologies and models employed by previous research contributions generally did not account for the effect, the size of a fund management company (measured by total AUM) could potentially have on the dynamics of flow-performance relationships. Thus the subsequent research question has additionally been deduced: Do outperforming funds of large international fund management companies (measured by the firm's AUM) experience an unproportionally larger amount of fund inflows than funds of highly specialized boutique fund management companies do?

Hypothesis 3

As the introductory chapter 1.1. has outlined, fund marketing and media presence can have a potentially significant influence on investor decisions. Since it can be expected that larger (international) fund management companies have access to considerably increased financial[33] and thus also more powerful marketing resources, they should have a natural edge over smaller asset management companies when it comes to attracting inflows by means of such selling propositions

Additionally it is assumed that outperforming funds of large international fund management companies can allure an unproportionally larger amount of fund inflows due to their extensive sales network and experience (as opposed to highly specialized boutique fund management companies).

1.4. Set up & structure

This thesis consists of both (i) a theoretical introductory part that will structurally motivate and guide the reader into the topic and its related fields of knowledge[34] and (ii) an extensive empirical part (performing a broad set of quantitative analyses), which will form the foundation of this thesis as this part will be delivering the

---

[32] Ber et al. (2007) also incorporated fund family size effects within their regression models.

[33] Fund management companies are mainly financing themselves through the management fee, an annually charged percentage of AUM. Thus a larger AUM directly relates into a increased management fee income.

[34] E.g. providing a short recap on the purpose and concept of mutual funds, the current structure of the mutual fund market as well as potential future industry threats.

inputs necessary for challenging the proposed hypothesis. Thus both parts are employing highly different methodologies and knowledge sources. While part one generally relies on making use of various different kinds of scientifically relevant (primary) literature, part two is processing an extensive sample of historical data by employing a set of quantitative models that are mainly based on the approaches of comparable research works. In more detail the two main segments of this thesis are designed as follows:

(i) The theoretical introductory part one comprises chapters 2-4 and is structured as follows: chapter 2 provides foundational insights into the concept and purpose of mutual funds in general. Moreover it also contains details about the historical and current structure of the global mutual fund market (with a strong focus on the European mutual fund industry). Regardless of the fact that chapter 2 is largely relying on theoretical concepts it is still seeking to add refreshing, discrete contributions whenever possible (e.g. by analyzing market-structures through independently conducted Gini-coeffcient tests).
Chapter 3 will then go more into detail and discloses common practices of how investors can actually assess and interpret a mutual fund's performance as well as risk figures. Besides general principles regarding the methodology and calculation of performance- and risk-figures, a considerable part of chapter 3 is devoted to the (time-wise) persistence of these measurement values. Although there are numerous performance and risk figures available for evaluating mutual funds, focus is clearly put on the most common measures that will also be incorporated in the later following flow-performance models. Eventually, the final pages of chapter 3 are delivering condensed insights on available life-cycle theories (based on empirical studies) for mutual funds – with particular focus on fund (net) flow attraction over time.
Previous research generally detected that (even though performance might not be persistent) a statistically significant correlation between past performance and lagged fund (net) flows is undeniable. In order to also be able to better understand herewith related psychological aspects of investor decisions chapter 4 is presenting findings of behavioral-finance research that has been dealing with mutual fund investment decisions and investment decisions in general.

(ii) The empirical part of this thesis (covering chapters 5-7) is aiming to answer all raised research questions by availing oneself of extensive historical track records for a selected sample of mutual funds, which are then processed by a set of quantitative models.

Chapter 5 starts off by providing comprehensive insights into the employed methodology – ranging from (i) a detailed description of how the sample has been derived, (ii) a presentation of (common) summary statistics, (iii) how the sample has subsequently been prepared. This is followed by thorough information on all the quantitative models that are being employed within this thesis. The exact set of model types is as follows:

- Rolling correlation analysis (Spearman's rank correlation)
- Bivariate OLS-regression models
- Piecewise bivariate OLS-regression models
- Multivariate OLS-regression models

Results of all the conducted statistical tests (including tests for significance) are then being presented in the subsequent chapter 6. The remaining chapter 7 will then seek to put all model-related findings into context for the sake of eventually being able to answer the raised research questions and to test all proposed hypotheses. Eventually a conclusion will discuss (i) which implications the results and findings of this thesis are demonstrating in context with the results of previous research and (ii) what additional worth-researching aspects this thesis has uncovered for potential future studies.

1.5. Primary sources

As chapter 1.4. has just presented in detail, this thesis is separated into one rather theoretical part and one quantitative empirical part. Thus also the primary sources of this thesis can roughly be segmented into (i) qualitative sources (primarily used for the theoretical part) and (ii) quantitative sources (used for the quantitative empirical part):

(i) Qualitative sources:

Qualitative sources have been used as the main input factor for the theoretical part (i) of this thesis and can further be divided into two segments. Segment one comprises well-established primary economics literature (Reilly (1994) as an example), which has mainly been used as a reference for generally valid (timeless) definitions and principles within the mutual fund industry. In order to also incorporate more current developments within the mutual fund industry and the flow-performance research in particular, this thesis is furthermore heavily reliant on the processing of working papers, articles from (industry relevant) trades journals or reports as well as studies from acknowledged industry research providers. These sources constitute the second segment of qualitative sources and have mainly been detected under the usage of top-tier research databases, such as the "ProQuest"- or "SSRN"- database.

(ii) Quantitative sources

Since this thesis is not just performing a straight forward literature review, but also seeks to add an innovative research contribution by performing its own quantitative empirical analyses, the employment of quantitative sources is playing a central role. By the term "quantitative sources" the author understands all input factors that have been necessary in order to develop and subsequently run all quantitative models.

From a model development point of view, this thesis is largely building up on the proven and tested model methodology of related research works (a detailed review of major contributions in the flow-performance research field is provided in chapter 1.2.). In order to guarantee a certain minimum level of quality, the author has decided to only consider referencing those research works that have been published in a top-tier trade journal (e.g. "Journal of Banking & Finance). General references regarding statistical principles as well as measurement methods for evaluating mutual fund performance have either been made from established primary-literature or the respective, directly underlying pioneer works (e.g. Sharpe (1966)).

With respect to the source of all actual quantitative data (i.e. historical track records for a sample of mutual funds) that is being processed in the various model types, the author has been granted permission to retrieve time series from the (usually not publicly accessible) Thomson Reuters database "Lipper for Investment Managers" (LIM). The actual model computations and executions are being performed by employing "Microsoft Excel" as well as the open-source programming language "R".

2. Properties of the mutual fund industry

Instead of starting with the quantitative empirical part right away, the following three chapters (chapters 2 to 4) will create context by delivering a useful and logically structured top-down information framework on the (for this thesis) most relevant key-aspects of mutual fund investing.

Due to the top-down approach of the "information framework" (comprising chapters 2 to 4) this first part (chapter 2) is designed to provide condensed insights into the market structure of today's mutual fund industry, without neglecting its past development as well potential future prospects (e.g. anticipated impacts of ongoing ETF-innovation and propagation). Even though some aspects might be valid for the global mutual fund industry also, the author puts strong emphasis on highlighting the situation for the European mutual fund industry (which will also be part of the quantitative empirical parts of chapters 5 to 7). Chapter 3 will then discuss how investors could (objectively) assess, compare and classify mutual funds and their (out-) performance, whereas chapter 4 will discuss how investors actually incorporate such measurement methods in their investment process.

2.1. Properties of mutual funds

Before directly going into the details of the key-properties of present-day mutual fund industries, it is beneficial to shortly recap the main purpose of the concept itself ("mutual funds") and to assess its justification for existence.

2.1.1. Purpose and benefits of mutual funds

One of the main ideas of the concept of mutual funds is to offer investors the advantage of accessing the benefits of a (usually) broadly diversified as well professionally managed portfolio at clearly reduced entry barriers. Thus by exploiting the concept of mutual funds also smaller investors have the possibility to easily diversify their capital across virtually any desired market, region or asset class.[35]

As it was already stated it the previous paragraph, mutual funds are managed professionally. Hence via employing mutual funds investors can in a sense "outsource" all or at least some parts of their personal asset allocation and portfolio

---

[35] HSBC (2005) pp. 52-54.

management decisions against a specific fee (management fee). So in contrast to direct participants of the respective underlying market (e.g. global equity market in case of global equity funds), mutual fund investors not necessarily need to permanently follow and react to new market information and movements as the fund management team takes care of such tasks.[36]

2.1.2. Active versus passive mutual funds

Although mutual funds can be classified in innumerable different ways, one rather foundational way of classification is the distinction between actively and passively managed mutual funds. This separative factor is highly essential as it usually acts as a strong explanatory factor for both performance objectives and fee structures of mutual funds.[37]

Depending on the respective asset class, passively managed mutual funds aim to track a certain market (e.g. by trying to mirror a certain index) whereas actively managed mutual funds usually communicate the objective of "beating" a certain market (respectively index). Another major difference between actively and passively managed funds is their fee/cost structure. Since passively managed funds simply need to track the performance of a certain target index (e.g. via constantly rebalancing the respective index holdings)[38], management of such funds usually involves considerably lower overhead-costs which should generally also lead to comparably lower management fees. Active funds , however, tend to run extensive research networks in order to achieve the information necessary for outperforming a certain benchmark. Needless to say such fund management structures can produce significantly higher running costs and therefore leads to comparably higher management fees.[39]

Within the quantitative empirical part of this thesis only actively managed mutual funds will become part of the researched sample (see chapter 5 "Methodology & definitions).

---

[36] HSBC (2005) pp. 19-20.

[37] SEC (2007) online.

[38] FINRA (2013) online.

[39] Edwin et al. (2009) pp. 703-704.

2.1.3. Open-ended versus closed-end funds

Another relatively foundational and (for the aims of this thesis) highly relevant way of separating investment funds is to distinguish between open-end and closed-end funds.

Closed-end funds are investment companies that issue a specified amount of shares to investors in the course of their initial public offering (IPO). After an IPO of a closed-end fund has taken place, the fund management company is usually neither willing to accept the issuance of new shares (which would directly lead to an increasing fund volume) nor the direct redemption of existing outstanding shares (which would directly lead to a decreasing fund volume). However, just as with ordinary equities, investors have the possibility to constantly trade shares on a secondary market.[40]

An open-end fund is the term for a set-up type of an investment company that is actually employed by most of those funds that are being commonly referred to as "mutual funds". In contrast to closed-end funds, open-end funds are explicitly willing to respond to changes in demand from new or existing investors by standing ready to issue or buy-back shares at virtually any time. Thus fund volume of open-end funds is not just dependent on a fund's portfolio performance (positive performance increasing the Net Asset Value (NAV)[41] and vice versa) but can also constantly be heavily affected by fund inflows and outflows as investors have the hypothetical possibility of pulling as much money in or out of the fund as they wish to do.[42]

Since closed-end funds are not willing (or able[43]) to let their fund volume be exposed to investor in- and outflows, only open-end funds will become part of the quantitative research part of this thesis (see chapters 5 to 7).

---

[40] Reilly (1994) p. 880.

[41] NAV equals the price of one unit (share) of a fund.

[42] Reilly (1994) p. 884.

[43] Closed-end funds might be invested in illiquid "niche-strategies".

2.1.4. Justification for existence

Chapter 2.1.1. already briefly stated the most evident benefits of the concept of mutual funds that can now be summarized as (i) enabling investors to achieve a diversified portfolio already with small capital amounts and (ii) offering a relatively cheap and easily accessible way to professional portfolio management.[44] Although over the past decades the benefits of mutual fund investments have clearly been extensively exploited by investors around the globe (see subsequent chapter 2.2 "Market development and competition" for details), today's mutual fund industry, and more specifically, actively managed mutual funds are far away from possessing an undisputed or not interchangeable function in global financial markets. The reasons for the currently highly questioned usefulness[45] as well as future of the (active) mutual fund industry can also be segmented into two (strongly interrelated) areas that are now being simplified as endogenous and exogenous factors:

(i) Endogenous factors: As chapter 3.2. will discuss and present in more detail, actively managed funds, on average, fail to beat their target market (benchmark) on a long-term perspective and thus only depict strongly limited persistence in performance.

(ii) Exogenous factors: Continuously increasing financial innovation in form of exchange traded funds (ETFs) has become a serious factor within the global fund industry.[46] Whereas some 20 years ago[47] investors would have only had the realistic[48] possibility to access a broadly diversified market or index by buying a suitable mutual fund (passive or active), they can now easily access a multitude of indices and markets by purchasing passive ETF-structures at considerably lower costs.

Combining both factors, the currently challenging situation for the (active) fund management becomes even more undeniable: A not very convincing average performance of actively managed funds in conjunction with comparably high man-

---

[44] HSBC (2005) pp. 19-20.

[45] Edwin et al. (2009) pp. 703-704.

[46] Reuters (2009) online.

[47] In 1993 State Street Global Advisors have launched the first ETF (passive ETF on the S&P 500).

[48] It is highly unlikely that a (smaller) investor seeks to follow a larger index (e.g. S&P 500) by directly acquiring all underlying index-constituents.

agement fees of active funds can potentially tempt investors to switch to competing cheaper products (e.g. ETFs or ordinary passive, index-funds).

2.2. Market development and competition

The following subchapter starts off by discussing the market size development of both the global and European mutual fund industry by presenting condensed empirical data taken from acknowledged industry sources (Investment Company Institute (ICI) in case of global market developments, European Fund and Asset Management Association (EFAMA) and Lipper for Investment Management (LIM) in case of the European market). This is followed by a structured evaluation of the current level of competiveness within the European mutual fund industry.

2.2.1. Market size and development: Global

The Investment Company Institute (ICI) is primarily known for its function as the "national association of U.S. investment companies (including mutual funds, closed-end funds, exchange-traded funds (ETFs) and unit investment trusts (UITs)"[49] and is therefore focused on publishing US-market related statistics. However, ICI also releases quarterly statistics on the global mutual fund industry on behalf of the International Investment Fund Association (IIFA).

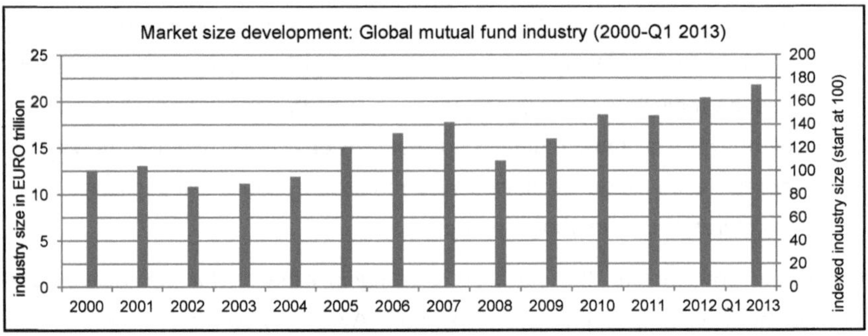

Illustration 1: Market size development: Global mutual fund industry (2000 – Q1 2013)

Just as the previous chart depicts, time series of historical data on worldwide market size provided by ICI are currently being available from the end of the year 2000 up to the end of the first quarter of 2013.[50]

---

[49] ICI a, (n.a.) online.

[50] ICI b, (n.a.) online.

According to the latest quarterly data compiled by the ICI, the global[51] mutual fund industry amounted to an all time-high of €21.75 trillion at the end of March 2013 (Q1 2013). When compared with the first available industry size data of end of 2000 (€12.60 trillion) the global mutual fund industry has grown by 72.60 % during that period (in nominal terms). However, industry growth within that period has been anything but monotonously increasing. Illustration 1 clearly reveals that most of the industry growth has been achieved within the recent four to five years, since the devastating effects of the financial crisis of 2008 almost caused the industry size to reach an all-time low (€13.60 trillion industry size by the end of 2008).

Although the above data is supposed to display the picture of a global mutual fund industry, a simple analysis (breakdown of the industry's total assets by domicile country) demonstrates the current level of geographical concentration. Based on ICI global market volume of Q1 2013 (€21.75 trillion) not less than 75.05 % of worldwide mutual fund assets can be attributed to the top 5 domiciles (in descending order: United States, Luxembourg, Australia, France and Ireland), with the US alone already accounting for 49.09 % of the industry.[52]

When analyzing the latest available industry size (Q1 2013) on basis of types of funds (or "asset classes"), the picture is as follows: 41.34 % of all industry assets can be allocated to equity funds, followed by bond funds (25.92 %), money market funds (16.73 %) and balanced/mixed funds with 11.76 % of market share.[53] According to ICI the remaining delta of 4.26 % can be allotted to "other" fund types as well unclassified funds.[54]

While the global data samples provided by ICI would actually allow for a multitude of further testing and evaluations, those opportunities are not exploited until the subsequent sub-chapter, which will explicitly highlight and analyze the current as well as past development of European mutual fund market.

---

[51] ICI consolidates data from national mutual fund associations of 45 different countries.

[52] ICI a, (2013) online.

[53] ICI b, (2013) online.

[54] ICI b, (2013) online.

2.2.2. Market size and development: Europe

A detailed and thorough analysis of the market framework of the European mutual fund industry is of particular interest for this thesis, as the quantitative empirical part (chapters 5 to 7) is strongly focusing on funds being domiciled within Europe. Moreover since the majority of comparable research (for more information please see chapter 1.2.) has been carried out for the US-American fund market, this sub-chapter will strongly concentrate on carving out characteristics that are unique to the European mutual fund industry.

Official statistics on the European mutual fund market and its size are published by the European Fund and Asset Management Association (EFAMA) on a monthly basis.[55] EFAMA can be considered as the European equivalent of IIFA and therefore acts as a cross-border representative association for 26 full-member countries and one observing country (Malta)[56], leading to a total sample of 27 European fund domiciles that are covered in EFAMA statistics. The following chart shows the historical market size development of the European mutual fund industry.

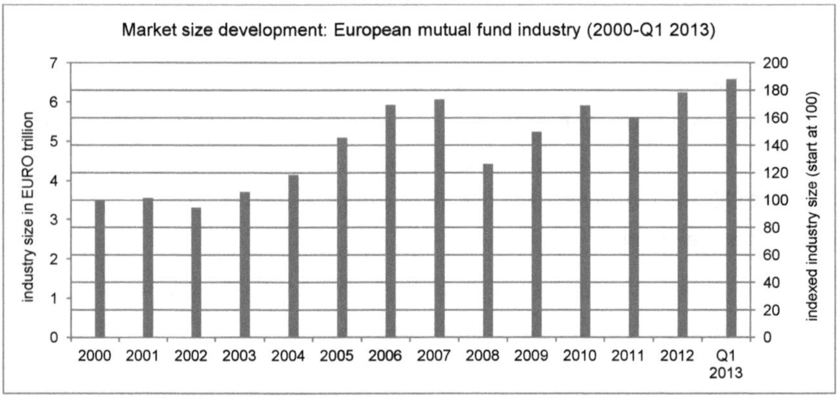

Illustration 2: Market size development: European mutual fund industry (2000 – Q1 2013)

For reasons of convenience[57] and consistency, the processed industry figures (Illustration 2) for the European market have also been taken from the comprehensive global mutual fund industry statistics provided by ICI. However, since

[55] EFAMA a, (2013) online.

[56] EFAMA b, (2013) online.

[57] EFAMA only publishes PDF-statistics; ICI also offers convenient xls-files.

EFAMA does not cover the Russian market in its statistics[58], this constituent has been removed from the European data sample in order to achieve homogeneity with EFAMA methodology (which is essential for further analyses).

Based on ICI data, the European domicile currently controls assets in the amount of € 6.6 trillion (as per Q1 2013). This means that, within the presented observation period (End 2000 until Q1 2013), the European mutual fund market has been able to almost double its industry volume (+ 88.14 % in nominal terms). However, it is not entirely meaningful to contrast this figure with the global growth figure presented in chapter 2.2.1. as it is largely biased by European data (as per Q1 2013 Europe had a 30 % share in the global mutual fund market).[59] Thus, in order to enable a more significant comparison, the subsequent chart compares the size development of both the European market and the adjusted "global (ex. Europe)" industry. For the sake of enhancing comparability, both industry sizes start at an indexed value of 100 in t=0 (2000).

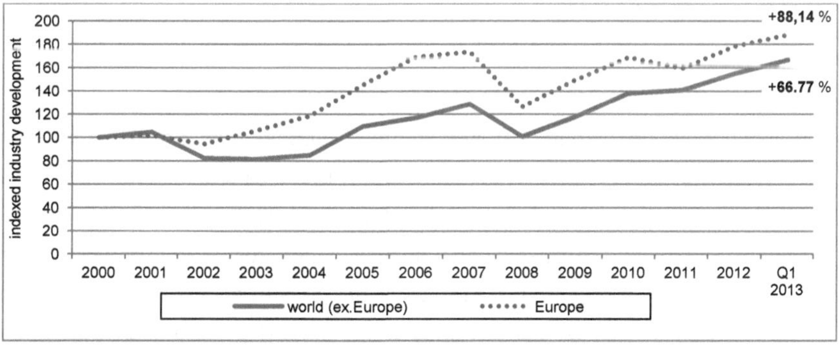

Illustration 3: Industry growth comparison: Europe versus Global (ex. Europe)

In addition to an obvious correlation between both samples (correlation coefficient close to 0.9), the above chart also discloses the outperformance, the European market has been able to achieve relative to the remaining global industry in terms of total growth rate within the observation period (88.15 % in the case of Europe versus +66.77 % in the case of the remaining global industry).

---

[58] EFAMA c, (2013) p. 9.

[59] ICI b, (2013) online.

Similar to the global market, also the European mutual fund industry can be characterized by exhibiting significant levels of geographical concentration. As per Q1 2013 a cumulated market share of 66.19 % could be attributed to the Top-3 domiciles (in descending order: Luxembourg, France and Ireland). The subsequent Lorenz curve visualizes the current level of geographical concentration.

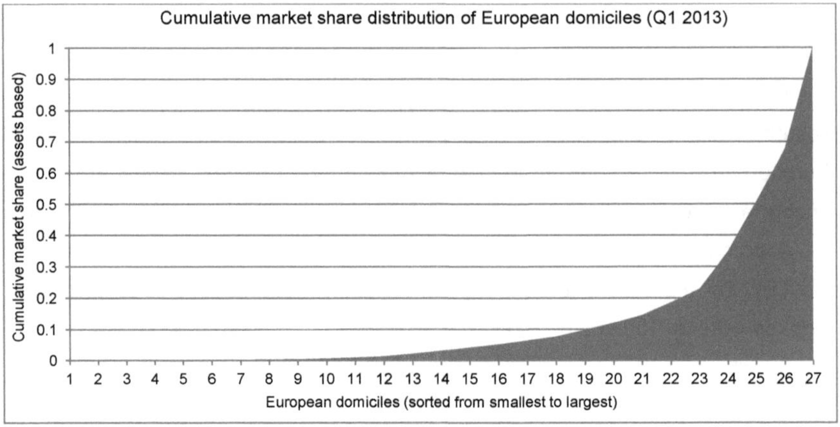

Illustration 4: Cumulative market share distribution of European domiciles (Q1 2013).

The above chart clearly demonstrates that the European fund industry is far from being equally distributed over all 27 domiciles. This is supported by the results of a Gini index calculation, which based on the data of Q1 2013, produces a Gini coefficient of 0.7678. Gini coefficients can potentially range from 0 (total equality) up to 1 (total inequality). In order to test this coefficient for consistency and to be able to research developments as well as trends in the underlying distribution, the author has additionally performed Gini calculations for historical points in time (2006 – Q1 2013).

The results of the historical Gini coefficient calculations are plotted in Illustration 5. It is observable that the level of inequality (Gini coefficient) remains relatively stable within the observed period (bandwidth of Gini coefficients ranging from 0.7251 in 2006 up to 0.7678 in Q1 2013). The highest annual change in inequality can be observed for the year 2008 with a relative increase in the Gini coefficient of +3.81 % (Gini 2007: 0.7291, Gini 2008: 0.7570) thus indicating that the financial crisis of

2008 generally fortified the geographical concentration within the European fund industry.

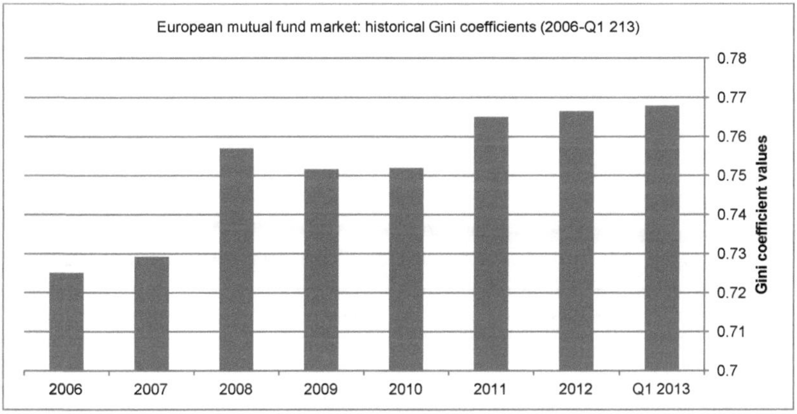

Illustration 5: European mutual fund market: historical Gini coefficients (2006-Q1 2013)

In respect to the top European domiciles, it has to be mentioned that the current no. 1 (Luxembourg) as well as no. 3 (Ireland) play a very specific role within the European (or even global) mutual fund industry. Both fund domiciles were able to significantly attract fund management companies over the past (see illustration 6), which is primarily a result of their relatively low levels of taxation ("tax havens") in connection with their capability to easily host "cross-border" UCITS fund structures. Once a UCITS ("Undertakings for Collective Investment in Transferable") structure is domiciled in an EU member country, the fund can easily be distributed across the remaining EU by applying the "passport" regulation.[60] Thus it can be argued that funds domiciled in Luxembourg or Ireland are typically not aiming to reach domestic investors but to simply exploit the above stated regulatory benefits.[61]

The subsequent chart highlights the increasing popularity of choosing European tax havens (Ireland and Luxembourg) as the fund domicile of choice. In order to enhance comparability, all industry sizes once again start at an indexed value of 100.

---

[60] SEI (2013) online.

[61] CACEIS (2011) pp. 22-26.

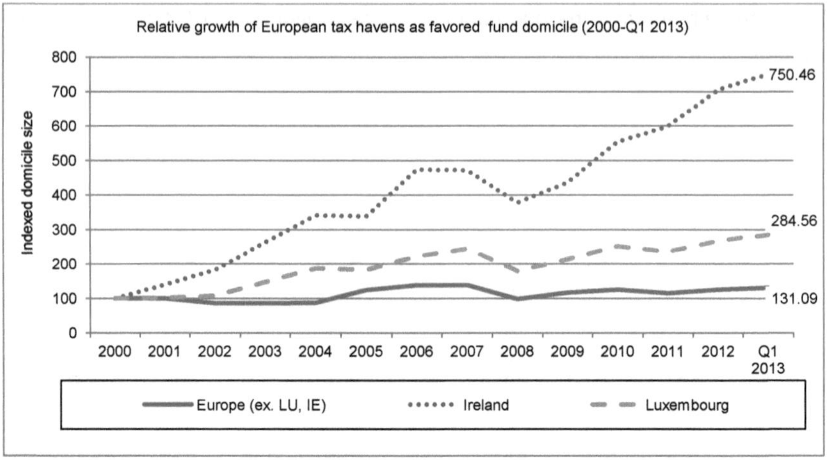

Illustration 6: Relative growth of European tax havens as favored fund domicile (2000-Q1 2013)

With fund industries growing by factors of 7.5 (Ireland) and 2.8 (Luxembourg) it is clearly recognizable that both "off-shore"" domiciles have been able to significantly outperform the remaining European domiciles (growth factor of 1.3). Having said that, it has to be mentioned that Irelands growth figure contains some bias since, at the starting point of this time series (2000), Luxembourg has already represented the largest European fund domicile (€ 792,781 million industry size according to ICI[62]), whereas back then Ireland only ranked as the seventh largest European fund domicile (€ 145,399 million domicile size).

2.2.3. Competition within the European fund industry

Since both ICI and EFAMA only deliver aggregated statistics based on relatively broad criteria (e.g. no data on sub-asset classes or fund management companies), the following sub-chapter will deliver an overview of the competitive situation within the European fund industry by making use of the highly detailed and comprehensive "Lipper for Investment Management" database, which will also be delivering the underlying time-series of the quantitative empirical part of this thesis (chapters 5 to 7).

[62] ICI (2005) p. 2.

Based on a Lipper database query of September 23, 2013 a total number of 33,414 funds (only primary tranches) is currently registered for distribution in at least one European country. When also taking into account multiple share-classes (e.g. distributing share classes or share classes in other currencies) this value instantly increases to 69,253 available funds.

As per September 23, 2013 the aggregated volume of all available primary tranches[63] amounts to € 4,742,324.74 million, respectively € 6,739,752.74 million when taking into account all available tranches. Please note that these figures differ from the statistics published by ICI and EFAMA due to (i) a different valuation date and (ii) the fact that also funds with a non-European domicile (e.g. US) can potentially be registered for distribution in a European country. Combining the number and volume of funds we receive an average fund size[64] of € 141.93 million for all primaries, and € 101.15 million when including all tranches, thus indicating that the majority of fund volume is typically located in the primary tranche, which is in line with the findings of comparable previous research work.[65]

The subsequent table provides descriptive statistics on the researched database sample (all open-ended mutual funds registered for distribution in Europe).

Summary statistics: Mutual fund size of researched sample (in EURm)

Tranches:	Primary	All tranches
Minimum:	0.00	0.00
1st Quantil:	6.84	2.71
Median	25.16	14.18
Mean	141.93	101.15
3rd Quantil:	91.78	59.00
Maximum:	50,542.44	50,542.44

Source: Lipper for Investment Management

Table 1: Summary statistics for mutual funds with European sales registration

Based on Lipper data exports, the above mentioned cumulated market volume can currently be attributed to 3,023 different fund management companies (3,067

63 Primary tranches are defined by the respective fund management company and typically comprise the majority of a fund strategy's volume. See for instance Ferreira et al. (2012) p. 1761.

64 Arithmetic mean.

65 E.g. Ferreira et al. (2012) p. 1761. (see chapter 1.2 for additional details on comparable research works).

when also taking into account fund management companies that currently do not report any volume). Based on the arithmetic average the typical fund management company is managing a total volume of € 2,227.49 million, whereas a median calculation produces a value of € 130.68 million. Since this value (median) is significantly lower than the arithmetic average, we can expect the underlying fund management volume distribution to be negatively skewed.

Summary statistics for assets under management of European fund management companies are provided in the subsequent table:

Summary statistics: Size of European fund management companies (EURm)

Minimum:	0.03
1st Quantil:	25.59
Median	130.68
Mean	2,227.49
3rd Quantil:	753.50
Maximum:	177,313.78

Source: Lipper for Investment Management

Table 2: Summary statistics for European fund management companies

Measuring the current level of inequality via a Gini index results in a considerably high Gini coefficient of 0.8844, the herewith related Lorenz curve is plotted in the subsequent chart.

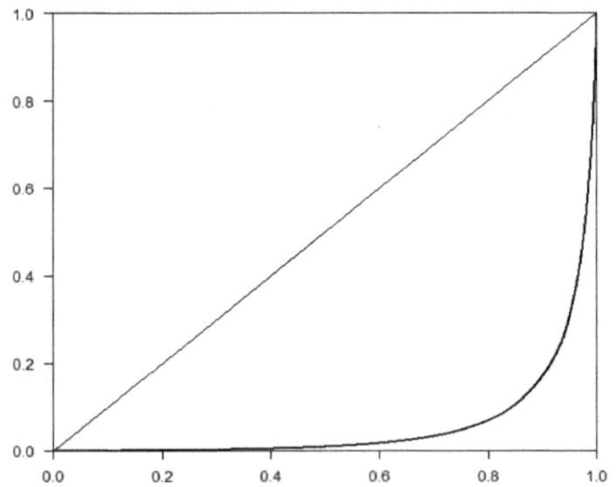

Illustration 7: Lorenz curve: Volume distribution of European mutual fund companies

Similar to the findings of chapter 2.2.2., illustration 7 further underscores the current level of concentration within the European mutual fund market, but this time from a fund management company's point of view. Based on the researched sample the 5 largest fund management companies (JPMorgan Asset Management (Europe) Sarl, Amundi SA, Franklin Templeton Investment Funds, BlackRock (Luxembourg) SA, PIMCO Global Advisors (Ireland) Ltd), are currently controlling 9.58 % of the European mutual fund market. These findings are of considerable interest for the remaining parts of this thesis, as it can be expected that such "big-players" have access to a significantly larger variety of distribution possibilities than smaller, or "ordinary" fund management companies do.

As per September 22, 2013 the market could be grouped into 14 different ("Lipper Global") major asset classes, and 353 sub-asset classes, ranging from "Absolute Return AUD High" to "Undisclosed". "Equity" ranks as the largest major asset class by volume (€ 2,240,609.29 million) and also ranks as the largest major asset class by fund count (11,375 equity funds as per September 22, 2013).[66]

The following table presents the respective market shares of the 14 major asset classes:

Assetclass	Fund count	Market share %	Volume (EURm)	Market share %	Avg. fund size
Equity	11,375	34.04%	€ 1,588,421.79	33.49%	€ 139.64
Bond	6,285	18.81%	€ 1,005,187.24	21.20%	€ 159.93
Money Market	1,588	4.75%	€ 751,628.28	15.85%	€ 473.32
Mixed Asset	6,752	20.21%	€ 703,689.94	14.84%	€ 104.22
Real Estate	632	1.89%	€ 165,362.73	3.49%	€ 261.65
Absolute Return	871	2.61%	€ 146,894.35	3.10%	€ 168.65
Hedge	1,336	4.00%	€ 139,787.56	2.95%	€ 104.63
Guaranteed	883	2.64%	€ 74,583.33	1.57%	€ 84.47
Target Maturity	584	1.75%	€ 53,916.20	1.14%	€ 92.32
Alternative	837	2.50%	€ 36,998.55	0.78%	€ 44.20
Protected	1,342	4.02%	€ 32,938.49	0.69%	€ 24.54
Unclassified	631	1.89%	€ 28,981.87	0.61%	€ 45.93
Commodity	256	0.77%	€ 11,759.55	0.25%	€ 45.94
Undisclosed	42	0.13%	€ 2,174.86	0.05%	€ 51.78
Total	**33,414**	**100%**	**€ 4,742,324.74**	**100%**	**€ 141.93**

Table 3: Market share of Lipper Global asset classes

It is noticeable that there can occur quite some divergences regarding market shares (i) measured in terms of fund count and (ii) measured in terms of volume of an asset class, implying that funds of some asset classes are able to manage a

[66] Only taking into account funds marked as „primary".

potentially larger average volume than funds of other (major) asset classes (e.g. "Equity"). Since fund managers are usually remunerated in a percentage of the fund's volume ("management fee")[67], this finding is of particular importance.

When applying the above analysis on a sub-asset class level, results are as follows: "Money Market EUR" currently ranks as the largest sub-asset class by volume (€346,267.70 million), whereas "Equity Global" ranks as the largest major asset class by fund count (2,288 Equity Global funds).[68]

The current top-10 sub-asset classes (as well as their cumulative market share) based on (i) asset class volume and (ii) fund count within the asset class are displayed in the consecutive table.

Assetclass	Volume (EURm)	Market share %	Fund count	Market share %
Money Market EUR	€ 346,267.70	7.30%	693	2.07%
Equity Global	€ 329,574.48	6.95%	2,288	6.85%
Money Market USD	€ 167,722.15	3.54%	182	0.54%
Bond Global	€ 142,145.50	3.00%	868	2.60%
Equity UK	€ 139,258.06	2.94%	357	1.07%
Equity Europe	€ 134,149.12	2.83%	1,126	3.37%
Money Market GBP	€ 121,670.73	2.57%	88	0.26%
Mixed Asset EUR Flex - Global	€ 120,758.64	2.55%	1,597	4.78%
Equity US	€ 110,423.98	2.33%	716	2.14%
Equity Emerging Mkts Global	€ 103,516.98	2.18%	629	1.88%
Top-10	**€ 1,715,487.34**	**36.17%**	**8,544**	**25.57%**
Total (449 assetclasses)	**€ 4,742,324.74**	**100.00%**	**33,414**	**100.00%**

Table 4: Market share of Top-10 sub-asset classes (only taking into account primary tranches)

2.3. Economies of scale

A fairly important question in connection with the overall aims of this thesis is to shortly recap, (i) why mutual funds actually strive to constantly increase their assets under management ("AUM" or fund volume) and (ii) which potential impacts an increase in fund volume can produce in terms of economies of scale effects.

(i) Mutual fund management companies generally desire an increasing fund volume due to the fact that the major part of their income is based on the management fee, a variable payment of a mutual fund investor that is linked to the respective volume of a fund. Another herewith directly related factor is profit maximization. Previous research has already well documented that there is a significant negative relation between a fund's size and its expendi-

[67] SEC (2013) online.

[68] Also only considering „primary " tranches.

ture ratio, which directly implies that there are economies of scale within the administration of a fund.[69] Thus a larger fund volume is naturally not only favored but also actively pursued by fund management companies.

(ii) Apart from the purely beneficiary "side-effects" of an increase in assets under management stated in (i), there are also numerous research studies regarding the potential negative impacts that can come along with the growth of a fund. These papers generally focused on the relationship between fund size and lagged fund performance (relative to a peer-group). Chen et al. (2004) firstly produced an extensive regression-based research on this relation and concluded that there is significant negative correlation between a fund's size and its (lagged) performance, suggesting that mutual fund size does (to a certain degree) erode future performance. Moreover Chen et al. (2004) indentify that this effect is comparably stronger for less liquid market segments (e.g. equity funds in the small & mid cap section).[70] These findings are also consistent with the results of more current research on this particular relationship.[71]

2.4. Boutique versus large fund management companies

As it has already been mentioned in chapter 2.2.3., the European mutual fund industry can be characterized by an enormously high level of concentration regarding the distribution of assets under management (AUM) over fund management companies (see for example illustration 7 for a cumulative AUM distribution). This finding is of particular interest for this thesis, as it is expected that the total AUM of a fund management company has a potential impact on its ability to attract new fund flows. Therefore this sub-chapter will shortly define, what is meant by (i) "boutique fund management companies" and (ii) "large fund management companies".

(i) Boutique fund management companies are (highly) specialized asset managers that are mostly privately owned and are usually only offering a handful of products within a few (usually interrelated) asset classes. Those compa-

---

[69] Latzko (1998) p. 10.

[70] Chen et al. (2004) pp.1-2.

[71] E.g. Yan (2008).

nies are usually solely doing business in the investment management sector and therefore do not offer any other financial services (also not via a subsidiary or an otherwise related company). Moreover they are generally overseeing a comparatively smaller AUM-size, which should enable them a higher degree of flexibility.[72]

(ii) Within this thesis the term "large fund management companies" refers to the asset management subsidiaries or the "investment management arms" of large financial institutions (such as banks, insurance companies, pension funds or financial conglomerates). Thus, such asset management corporations are, in contrast to boutiques, not acting independently, but are rather largely being influenced by affiliated or parent companies.[73]

However, this dependence also enables them to easily access a large network of existing customers that seek to be served with mutual funds (e.g. clients of retail-banking or private banking branches).[74] As a result of this existing demand, this fund management company type is usually offering a highly comprehensive product range over a multitude of asset classes and is consequently also managing a relatively large AUM-size.[75]

Due to their integration in large financial groups and the herewith associated access to existing customer demand as well as to other important resources (e.g. know-how, IT-architectures, brand awareness, financial resources), this thesis is expecting "large fund management companies" to have an edge over boutiques in terms of gaining inflows from investors (see H3 in chapter 1.3. for details).

Since the majority of comparable research work has been carried out for the US American mutual fund market (e.g. Ippolito (1992), Sirri/Tufano (1993) or Chevalier/Ellison (1997)) it is essential to mention that the distribution of mutual funds is significantly more reliant on using banking branches as a sales channel for the European retail (and especially Europe (ex. UK)) market than it is for the US mu-

---

[72] Essvale Corporation Limited (2007) pp. 12-13.

[73] Essvale Corporation Limited (2007) pp. 11-13.

[74] Koch (2007) pp. 89-90.

[75] Essvale Corporation Limited (2007) pp. 11-13.

tual fund retail market. [76] Therefore possible deviations between the findings of this thesis (focusing on the European market) and the already carried out previous research (see chapter 1.2. for details) will also carefully be checked along this specific criterion.

[76] CACEIS (2011) p. 7.

3. Outperformance & performance persistence

In order to understand how and why investors are chasing past performance (and subsequently "outperformers)" it is vital to (i) elaborate the common ways of identifying and assessing outperformers and (ii) how persistent these assessments are in practice.

3.1. How to identify outperformers

As chapter 2.2.3. already disclosed, there are currently 33,414 mutual funds available for sale within the European continent (69,253 when not only accounting for primary share classes). Since it can be supposed that almost every single one of them publicly claims to pursue the ideal and most promising investment strategy, it is fairly reasonable to raise the question of how investors should actually scan and evaluate this comprehensive and not really transparent investment universe when planning a mutual fund investment.

3.1.1. Asset class classifications

Before blindly and non-structurally comparing mutual funds based on (past) performance figures it is vital so segment them based on similarities. One of the most foundational tasks in the process of mutual fund (performance) assessment is to group the potentially available investment universe (e.g. all mutual funds with sales registration in Europe) according to the underlying funds' asset classes. Although mutual funds themselves can also be considered an own asset class (in comparison to direct equity or bond investments), it is highly typical to apply this term within the mutual fund universe as well.

In the mutual fund industry the term generally refers to the respective focus of a mutual fund manager's communicated[77] investment strategy, with "focus" comprising several characteristics such as employed investment instruments (e.g. bond, equity, money market, real estate, convertibles, etc.), investment region (e.g. global, USA, Europe, Emerging Markets Asia), industry sector (e.g. pharmacy or basic industries). However, there is no generally (or globally) valid definition for

[77] A mutual fund's detailed investment strategy (and its limitations) is usually publicly communicated in the provided prospectus.

asset class classifications, which also explains why fund data providers (in this case Lipper for Investment Management and Morningstar) apply different asset class groupings.[78]

Even though asset class classifications are not uniform and might leave room for interpretation, they still offer investors a highly convenient way of indentifying a reasonably homogenous peer-group which can afterwards still be customized based on personal requirements.

3.1.2. Performance evaluation

Once the investor has identified a desired asset class and further homogenized the output-peer group based on personal minimum criteria (potentially comprising factors such as minimum track record or volume, fee-structure, domicile, sales registration, tax-status), the remaining "long-list" can be compared based on various (past) performance-, risk- as well as risk-adjusted performance figures.

Although the financial industry and academia has already come up with a highly comprehensive set of different quantitative evaluation figures with different levels of complexity and relevancy, this thesis focuses on researching the impact of three rather straight-forward measuring values: (i) percentage growth, (ii) volatility (standard deviation of returns) and (iii) Sharpe ratio (as a commonly used risk-adjusted performance figure). Thus, this sub-chapter will also only present these three evaluation principles. A concise summarized critical reflection of traditional wide-spread performance evaluation concepts is delivered in (iv).

(i) Percentage growth

Percentage growth is probably the most simple and thus might also one of the most misleading and featureless[79] performance figures within the financial industry. Still, as the introductory part of this thesis has already outlined, several mutual fund rankings are based on pure (non-risk adjusted) performance figures and thus might have an especially seductive impact on investor behavior.

---

[78] Lipper (2008) versus Morningstar (n.a.) online.

[79] If interpreted on an entirely isolated basis.

In concrete terms, percentage growth represents the relative change in a fund's Net Asset Value (NAV) that has been observed within a specific, pre-defined period[80]:

$$\text{percentage growth} = \frac{\text{NAV}_{t+1}}{\text{NAV}_{\text{t}}} - 1$$

Illustration 8: Calculation of percentage growth

Please note that, in order to increase comparability, the empirical part of this thesis employs percentage growth figures that are calculated on a total-return principle (i.e. assuming a reinvestment of all distributions (e.g. dividends) that have occurred within the respective observation period)[81].

Once the percentage growth figure has been calculated for the desired peer-group as well as the desired period, respectively interval (e.g. yearly-basis or year-to-date), the long-list can be ranked based on the observed results (e.g. via purely ordinal rankings or categorization into specific quantiles).

(ii) Volatility (standard deviation)

If interpreted on an entirely isolated basis, also the volatility (standard deviation) of a mutual fund or rather of a mutual fund's performance has strongly limited informative value. In mutual fund assessments volatility is typically measured as the square root of the sum of squared deviations between all observed monthly returns and the period's average monthly return (arithmetic mean)[82]:

$$\text{monthly volatility } \sigma = \sqrt{\sum_{i=1}^{n} \overline{(\text{MR} - \text{MR}_\text{i})^2}}$$

MR_i: Observed monthly return $\overline{\text{MR}}$: Arithmetic average of observed monthly returns

Illustration 9: Calculation of monthly volatility

Within this thesis all empirical work will be based on annualized standard deviations, which are simply achieved by multiplying monthly observations by the square root of 12.[83]

---

[80] AXA (2013) online.

[81] AXA (2013) online.

[82] Haslem (2010) pp. 165-166.

[83] Haslem (2010) p. 166.

Although standard deviation (or "volatility") is not telling anything about a fund's actual return (or whether it has been positive or negative), it is still revealing information about the level of fluctuation of a fund's achieved returns and thus its risk. In general investors are told to favor investments with a lower volatility as they are assumed to be less risky. However, just as in the case of evaluating mutual fund returns, standard deviation is only becoming meaningful when compared to other homogenously oriented funds (i.e. funds of the same asset class or peer group).[84]

(iii) Sharpe ratio

The Sharpe ratio principle combines both (i) and (ii) as it computes a single figure that incorporates the (excess[85]) return as well as the variability of returns (i.e. volatility) of an investment and thus serves investors as a wide-spread risk-adjusted performance figure.[86] In mutual fund terms, Sharpe ratio is calculated based on the following formula:

$$Sharpe\ ratio_{\mathrm{MF}} = \frac{\overline{\mathrm{R}}_{\mathrm{MF}} - \overline{\mathrm{R}}_{\mathrm{RF}}}{\sigma_{\mathrm{MF}}}$$

Illustration 10: Calculation of Sharpe ratio

Within the numerator of the above formula, $\overline{\mathrm{R}}_{\mathrm{MF}}$ denotes the observed mean return that a mutual fund has achieved over a certain set of observation periods (e.g. last 12-months) and $\overline{\mathrm{R}}_{\mathrm{RF}}$ stands for the mean return, an applicable seemingly risk-free reference-index (e.g. 3-month EURIBOR) has generated throughout the selected observation period(s). Thus $\overline{\mathrm{R}}_{\mathrm{MF}} - \overline{\mathrm{R}}_{\mathrm{RF}}$ computes the average excess return a mutual fund has been able to deliver versus a risk-free index. The denominator σ_{MF} is what actually produces the risk-adjusted "nature" of the Sharpe ratio as it integrates the standard deviation of a mutual fund's observed returns (and hence its risk). Consequently the Sharpe ratio measures the amount of excess return a mutual fund has earned per unit of taken risk.[87]

When comparing Sharpe ratios of mutual funds within one peer-group a higher Sharpe ratio is generally preferred (by risk-averse investors) as risk is or , in order

---

[84] Morningstar (2010) online.

[85] Versus a risk-free benchmark.

[86] Haslem (2010) p. 166.

[87] Reilly (1994) p. 949.

to account for the past oriented methodology of this concept, “has been” rewarded at a higher proportion. However, the concept of comparing Sharpe ratios has one highly significant drawback: Sharpe ratios only deliver meaningful outputs when the researched investments have delivered positive excess returns versus the risk-free benchmark. In the case of negative excess returns (i.e. losses or returns smaller than the risk-free investment) the concept becomes misleading as funds with a higher level of risk are suddenly getting rewarded with a higher Sharpe ratio.[88]

(iv) Drawbacks of traditional measures

One the most significant drawbacks of the just presented risk (adjusted) performance evaluation figures is actually based on the impacts of their greatest advantage: their simplicity. Due to their non-complex methodology these models are considerably simplifying the underlying input dynamics.
One example is the assumption that (mutual fund) returns are normally distributed which in fact is highly questioned by financial academia.[89] Since this thesis is only employing backward looking – actually observed historical performance figures, the assumption of normal distributions is not impacting results at all. However, for the sake of providing a bigger picture, it has to be mentioned that such model-specific and distributional assumptions are highly dangerous when being applied in a prospective way (such as the simulation of future results (e.g. via a GBM) or losses (e.g. VaR under the variance-covariance approach)).

Another major downside of all of the just presented, rather simple performance figures is the fact that they have either no or only absolutely limited informative value when not being put in an appropriate context. As an example: If historical Sharpe ratios of two randomly chosen mutual funds (fund A: 1-Y Sharpe ratio of 2, fund B: negative 1-Y Sharpe ratio) of two different asset classes are being evaluated – based on solely that information - one could not deduct that fund A has automatically been the “better” fund. Fund A might has been a US-equity fund that has been able to participate in a general bull market, but might still performed way worse than the majority of other peer-group constituents. On the other hand, fund

[88] Standard & Poor’s (2013) online.

[89] Haslem (2010) p. 166.

B might has been a THB-bond fund who had to follow a general bear market, but could still have been able to handle the market downswing much better than comparable (THB-bond) funds. Thus, just as chapter 3.1.1 has already outlined, a clear and meaningful asset class-, respectively peer-group classification is always needed before interpreting such one-dimensional performance figures.

However, it is not the aim of this thesis to question the functionality or usefulness of such traditional and wide-spread performance figures any further, but to simply deliver an empirical research on the impact such measures have on actual investor behavior (in terms of fund flows).

3.2. Persistence of mutual fund returns

As it has already been discussed quite broadly, the main problem with an investment's (traditional[90]) performance assessment and all the herewith related performance figures is the entire reliance on past data as input variables. However, since an investor is, not surprisingly, unable to invest in past track records it is just fair to question the persistence of mutual fund returns and associated performance and risk figures. In other words: Are past winners also likely to be future winners?

Since a multitude of various different research papers has already extensively researched the persistence of mutual fund returns and performance figures it is not necessary to carry out independent empirical, quantitative investigations on this matter, but to simply deliver a condensed meta-analysis of already carried-out research.

Pioneer work within this particular research field has been achieved by Sharpe (1966). On the final pages of his well-known publication in the "Journal of Business" he tests the predictability of his just-developed Sharpe ratio (or "Reward-to-Variability ratio" as it has been denoted back then) by measuring rank correlation between a mutual fund rankings[91] of two periods (1944-1953, 1954-1963). Sharpe argues to having indentified "a reasonable amount of consistency between both

[90] More complex models might also incorporate forward-looking qualitative factors (e.g. implementing the results of a professional due-diligence).

[91] Covering only a very small sample of 35 mutual funds.

periods".[92] However, only two years later Jensen (1968) has challenged performance persistence (based on the Jensen's alpha performance figure) by concluding that there is "very little evidence that any individual fund was able to do significantly better than that which we expect from mere random chance"[93].

One of the most foundational contributions in the field of mutual fund's return performance persistence has been achieved by Carhart (1997). In his publication in the Journal of Finance he researched the performance persistence of equity mutual funds by building equally weighted decile[94]-portfolios with annual rebalancing.[95]. Although Carhart detects some evidence for short-term (one-year persistence) he concludes that almost all of the persistence within mutual fund (risk-adjusted) performance is actually explained by "common factors in stock returns and investment expenses" and thus not by the abilities of extraordinarily skilled fund managers.[96] Another, for this thesis increasingly relevant, finding of Carhart is regarding the consistency in yearly-fund-rankings. Even when using yearly gross performance (and thus the just described impact of fee-persistence) he only detects that top-funds of the previous year are only "somewhat more likely to remain winners" (and vice-versa for last year's loser-funds). Based on this research only 20% of previous year's top-decile funds have been able to remain top-decile in the subsequent year as well.[97]

More recent studies have (as a result of technological progress) started to employ increasingly sophisticated models (generally incorporating time-varying parameters in their applied regression models) in order to measure performance persistence. They generally also focus on indentifying whether performance persistence of mutual fund managers is a result of skill or luck and mostly conclude that it is based on the latter. [98]

---

[92] Sharpe (1966) pp. 134-135.

[93] Jensen (1968) p. 415.

[94] Decile segmentation based on performance of previous (one- to five-year) periods.

[95] Carhart (1997). p. 75.

[96] Carhart (1997) p. 57.

[97] Carhart (1997) p. 71.

[98] Hereil et al. (2010) p. 2

Since a complete review of all available (acknowledged) research on performance persistence in the mutual fund industry would go beyond the scope of this thesis (as it could easily engage the writing of an own, dedicated thesis), the author will not discuss performance persistence issues any further. However, due to the (above presented) general tendencies towards findings that are supporting a non-persistence of mutual returns, the complete set of statistical models of the quantitative empirical part of this thesis (from chapter 5 onwards), as well as the interpretation of the herewith associated model outputs, is building upon the suggestions of Eugene Fama's efficient-market hypothesis (EHM) and thus assumes that mutual funds (or to be more precise: mutual fund managers) are not able to consistently outperform their reference market on a risk-adjusted basis.[99] A clear position against performance-consistency is vital for the remaining parts of this thesis, as doing otherwise would dramatically impact the interpretation of collected flow-performance-relationship test results.[100]

3.3. Life-cycle theory

With the exception of target-maturity funds, shares of open-ended mutual funds are (just like corporate equity) typically issued for an infinite period of time.[101] In praxis this "infinite maturity concept" can only be harmed through fund (full) closures or fund mergers.[102] Thus investors usually have access to an investment universe that is covering mutual funds with all kinds of different track record lengths, potentially ranging from zero (open-ended funds that are pre-IPO stage) up to several decades.

The undeniable track record variety that is available to (potential) mutual fund investors is causing two major questions to be discussed:

---

[99] Mayo (2008) pp. 299-300.

[100] In a world with clearly supporting indications for performance persistence and investors mostly following the suggestions of a homo economicus influenced behavior, a highly significant positive flow-performance relationship could actually be expected a priori, and thus would not really need any closer research.

[101] IMCA (2003) p. 177.

[102] Vanguard (2013) p. 1.

(i) How should mutual fund investors incorporate track record length within their investment process (in theory) and to what extent do empirical results support these theoretical principles?

(ii) Based on the findings of (i): How should this thesis account for track record variety within the quantitative empirical models?

Regarding question (i) a short literature review is disclosing that when it comes to picking and evaluating actively-managed mutual funds, investors are generally advised to prefer funds with long-term track records (mutual fund investing manuals are typically suggesting a minimum track record of 5-10 years[103]). A longer track record should typically be preferred as it is revealing insights on a mutual fund's (or to be more specific: a mutual fund manager's) performance consistency during different types of market-phases (e.g. performance in both bear and bull markets). However, the advantages of a long track record can easily be wiped out by the occurrence of fund manager changes.[104]

Having said that, actual investor behavior appears to largely be ignoring the above stated suggestions as studies have shown that investors are primarily focusing on a fund's last year performance[105] when conducting mutual fund investments, and thus are not paying too much attention on long-term track records.[106] Additionally, the quantitative (regression) models of previous contributors in the flow-performance research field have also examined the impact of adding a fund's age as a dependent variable and generally detected a statistically significant negative impact[107] – suggesting that (after having accounted for a broad set of other control variables) older funds do attract fund (net) flows at a lower rate than comparably younger funds.

The favoritism towards funds with long-term track records that is being proposed by advising literature[108] seems to be further ignored by investors in practice, when

---

[103] E.g. Khalfani (2004) p. 66. or Snelson/Graham (2008) p. 132.

[104] Snelson/Graham (2008) p. 132.

[105] Thus also the later following quantitative models of this thesis will employ one-year performance figures as input variables.

[106] Nofsinger (2002) p. 157.

[107] E.g. Ferreira et al. (2012) p. 1765. or Barber et al. (2005) p. 2106.

[108] E.g. Khalfani (2004) p. 66. or Snelson/Graham (2008) p. 132.

taking into account flows into new products. A study carried out by the globally acknowledged fund rating agency "Morningstar" has shown that newly released funds (by Morningstar definition the term "newly released funds" comprises all funds with a track record of less than one year) were able to attract approximately 60 % of cumulated mutual fund (net) flows that have been observed for the European market in the first half of 2013.[109] Although this figure only constitutes an industry snap-shot with limited informative value on long-term implications, it is still highly alarming that investors are actually capable of allocating such significant amounts towards new funds that are either only possessing a very short-term track record or even no track record at all.

With respect to question (ii) and in order to meaningfully process the above stated findings and suggestions in the later employed quantitative models of this thesis, the author has decided to follow the methodology of previous research and thus will also incorporate fund age as explanatory factor for fund flows in selected (multivariate) regressions.

---

[109] Morningstar (2013) online.

4. Investor behavior

The majority of comparable previous research works (chapter 1.2. provides a detailed review of comparable research contributions) detected that, even though there are no clear indications on performance persistence, there is statistically significant and positive correlation between mutual fund past performance and lagged fund (net) flows – indicating that investors let themselves be significantly steered by past performance, and by past short-term performance in particular.[110] Moreover these studies generally identified their underlying flow-performance relationships to be depicting a convex form, meaning that investors are strongly chasing past winners but are only very hardly getting rid of past losers. Based on such findings (and other rather illogical investor reactions that are being documented within this chapter), actual behavior of mutual fund investors appears to be far from being entirely rational. In order to be able to better explain indications for irrational investor behaviors that potentially could occur during the later following model executions, this chapter will deliver condensed insights into how behavioral finance research is generally documenting and justifying such investor reactions.

Sub-chapter 4.1. will quickly summarize some general findings of behavioral finance research studies that are of particular interest for the purposes and aims of this thesis and is furthermore discussing how behavioral finance is directly addressing to the set of mutual investor irrationalities that have been detected by previous flow-performance relationship research works. Sub-chapter 4.2. will then be disclosing how some of those already documented irrationalities can be accounted for in the later following quantitative models of this thesis.

4.1. Behavioral finance and the flow-performance relationship

As the opening part of this chapter has just outlined, mutual fund investor behavior is depicting strong signs for irrational behavior. This sub-chapter will structurally present the most relevant indications for investor irrationalities (based on the findings of (acknowledged) previous research publications) and discusses how behavioral finance research can be used as a possible explanation.

---

[110] Nofsinger (2002) p. 157.

Since a statistically significant positive flow-performance relationship has been identified by all previous research contributors that have been reviewed in course of chapter 1.2 (literature review), this finding constitutes the most prominent mutual fund investor behavior irrationality within the focused research field. But why do investors actually chase past-performance (and short-term past-performance in particular), if there are no clear indications for performance persistence? [111]

When approaching this question from a behavioral finance point of view, "recency bias" could be considered as a potentially explaining concept. This particular finding of behavioral finance studies is suggesting that investors are expecting the most recent past-developments to continue in future as well (i.e. a past outperforming fund is expected to also continue its outperformance in future).[112] Industry experts additionally mention a general lack of financial education of mutual fund investors as well as a potentially misleading layout of fund fact sheets (which are putting too much emphasis on past figures) as potentially explaining factors for this particular investor irrationality.[113]

Although the concept of "recency bias" can be considered as a valid explanation for the generally observed "performance chasing of investors", it is not really helping to explain the convex form of a mutual fund's flow-performance relationship that has been detected by the majority[114] of comparable previous research. The frequently identified flow-performance convexity is generally suggesting that underperforming funds are less sensitive towards fund (net) in- or outflows than outperforming funds (i.e. investors are (by means of fund flows) generally rewarding outperformers at a higher level than they are penalizing underperformers). However, based on a pure "recency bias" concept, investors should expect underperforming funds to keep performing baldy in the future as well and thus, one would generally have assumed that investors are also demonstrating a high degree of

---

[111] A detailed review of research on mutual fund performance persistence is performed in chapter 3.2..

[112] Pompian (2012) pp. 113-114.

[113] Fiduciary News (2013) online.

[114] Out of all reviewed research publication of chapter 1.2. Ferreira et al. (2012) represents the only constituent that did not receive a statistically significant convex for all researched samples.

sensitivity towards bad past-performance.[115] Based on behavioral finance research the flow-performance convexity can better be explained by the impacts of the "disposition effect". This concept (which has been proven by empirical studies on various market types) is suggesting that investors are perceiving investment losses to a much stronger extent than investment gains – which, in exaggerated formulation, is leading to the phenomenon that loss realization is being postponed as long as possible (partly also due to the fact that investors tend to consider loss realizations as being equal to admitting a wrong investment decision) whereas realization of investment wins cannot be achieved fast enough. In mutual fund terms this means that investors are exhibiting the tendency of holding on to mutual funds with bad performance for too long and selling winning funds too early.[116]

A high degree of significant autocorrelation between timely-lagged fund (net) flows is representing yet another irrational behavior of mutual fund investors that is frequently being detected by previous studies on flow-performance aspects.[117] Ber et al. (2007) are explaining such autocorrelations by mutual fund investors being exposed to a certain degree of a "status quo bias". In case of being exposed to such a kind of bias, investors are reluctant to switch investments even if switching to a different investment would result in an optimized outcome.[118]

4.2. Incorporating investor irrationalities in quantitative models

Since the identification of a significant positive and convex flow-performance relationship as well as the herewith associated investor biases ("recency bias" and "disposition effect") is considered as one of the potentially central findings of this thesis rather than a distortive and unwished effect, quantitative models will not seek to control for any of those two types of biases. However, similar to the methodologies of previous studies in the flow-performance relationship research also this thesis will account for a potentially significant autocorrelation between lagged fund flows within the later presented multivariate OLS-regression models by additionally incorporating past (net) flows as explanatory (control) variables.[119]

---

[115] Pompian (2012) pp. 113-114.

[116] Baker et al. (2010) pp. 527-528.

[117] E.g. Ferreira et al. (2012) p. 1765. or Ber et al. (2007) p. 20.

[118] Pompian (2012) pp. 40-41.

[119] E.g. Ferreira et al. (2012) p. 1765. or Ber et al. (2007) p. 20.

5. Methodology & definitions

The following three chapters represent the innovative core part of this thesis as they contain (i) the structured theoretical development of the necessary quantitative empirical models (presented in this chapter 5. "Methodology & definitions"), (ii) the actual application of the developed models on an extensive and highly representative historical data set (performed in chapter 6. "Time series analysis") and an eventual interpretation of the collected results along the proposed hypotheses (exhibited in chapter 7. "Empiric evidence").

This chapter will start off by stating the various types of data needed (and how and where they have been collected) in order to fulfill the tasks of the empirical part of this thesis (presented in 5.1.). Sub-chapter 5.2. will then present summary statistics of the collected data types and also discusses their representative character. Final sub-chapter (5.3.) contains details about the employed correlation and regression models.

5.1. Empirical set up

The subsequent sub-chapters provide structured insights into how the author has come up with the later on processed data sample by covering essential aspects such as: where all data exports are derived from (5.1.1. "Data source"), which historical time period(s) are included (5.1.2. "Data horizon and frequency"), which explicit criteria funds have to meet in order to become part of the sample (5.1.3. "Data focus") up to which specific key-variables (primarily focusing on performance-figures) of qualified funds are being included in the sample (5.1.4. "Required types").

5.1.1. Data source

All empirical data that is being processed within the upcoming quantitative models has been obtained from the extensive mutual fund data base "Lipper for Investment Management" (a subsidiary of the global information provider Thomson Reuters).[120] The database is not publicly accessible but involves a monthly subscription fee – however, the international research company "e-fundresearch.com Data

[120] Lipper (2013) online.

GmbH" has granted the author of this thesis to retrieve the necessary data via their account. The employed data base account is limited to all open-ended mutual funds that are (or have been) registered for distribution in at least one European[121] country. However, due to the fact that, compared to the US-mutual fund industry, the performance-flow relationship is still underresearched for the European market (see chapter 1.2. for details).

Lipper for Investment Management offers a multitude of qualitative data (e.g. fund names, ISIN, fund company names, asset classes, country registrations, domicile) as well as a variety of quantitative master data (e.g. reported fund volumes, NAVs) and an additional set of derived performance analytics (e.g. various performance, risk and risk-adjusted performance statistics).

5.1.2. Data horizon and frequency

One of the most significant drawbacks of so far produced comparable research is the fact, that they are only measuring static time frames (typically calendar years). For the sake of addressing this shortcoming and to significantly maximize the researched sample, the author has decided to calculate all models based on a monthly rolling one-year time-frame, thereby instantly achieving an increase in data points by factor x12.

The subsequently displayed chart illustrates the time-lag methodology that is being employed for all quantitative models of this thesis.

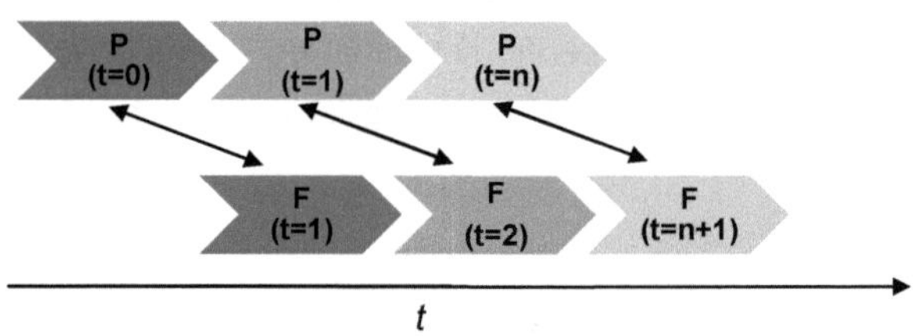

Illustration 11: Simplified demonstration of employed time-lag methodology

Whereas "P" denotes any kind of a mutual fund's observed performance-figure (e.g. observed annualized percentage growth, volatility or Sharpe ratio) that is being researched within the upcoming flow-performance correlation and regression models, "F" is representing a fund's observed, annual relative fund (net) flow. In

[121] For a detailed list of covered countries please refer to document D in the appendix.

order to create a certain kind of "causality-setting", both observation values are not being contrasted (e.g. via correlation or regression tests) simultaneously (i.e. P (t=0) versus F (t=0)), but are being compared by introducing a time-lag of one year (i.e. P (t=0) is contrasted against F (t=1)). In a more concrete example this means that a mutual fund's performance in the calendar year 2012 (e.g. Sharpe ratio of 1.5 as per 31.12.2012) is compared to its annual relative (net) fund flows that have been observed in the subsequently following one year period (e.g. relative fund (net) flows of +32% as per 31.12.2013). The just described time-lag methodology is consistent with acknowledged previous research contributors.[122]

Data collection starts at a valuation-date of 31st of August, 2003 for annual performance figures and 31st of August 2004 for annual fund net flows (in order to account for a lagged-relationship). Data collection ends at 31st of August, 2012 for annual performance figures and 31st of August, 2013 for annual flow values. Thus, a total number of 109 data points is researched for each key-variable of all included funds.

Similar to the methodology of the majority of comparable flow-performance relationship research studies, this thesis is also using a data set which is entirely free of survivorship-bias. Hence all employed models are also incorporating data of funds that have already ceased to exist up to current date.[123] Details on the exact number of liquidated mutual funds that have been included within the sample(s) are displayed in the summary statistics of sub-chapter 5.2.

5.1.3. Data focus & sample limitations

All required data has been obtained for a dynamic "Lipper for Investment Management" fund list which has been restricted based on the following criteria.

Geographical focus & sales distribution

As it has already shortly been discussed within the literature review part of this thesis (chapter 1.2.), previous research works in the flow-performance relationship

---

[122] E.g. Ber et al. (2007) or Ferreira et al. (2012).

[123] CAIA Association (2009) p. 240.

field generally focused on limiting their researched mutual fund sample by only taking to account funds of one domicile (e.g. only equity mutual funds with US-domicile). However, such a methodology is directly suggesting that only mutual fund managers that belong to the exact same fund domicile are competing against each other for investor inflows (or to limit outflows in negative market periods). While such a perception of mutual fund competition might be justifiable for a highly restrictive (geographical) mutual fund market, it is highly questionable for the European market, which possesses an increasingly transparent mutual fund market with considerable cross-border fund distributions.[124] Since this thesis is focusing on highlighting the case for the European mutual fund market, the entire methodology needs to account for cross-border activity and is thus not limiting its sample based on a mutual fund's domicile. Within the field of flow-performance relationship research, this thesis is therefore taking an alternative, rather innovative approach of limiting its fund sample – namely by sales registration. This means every mutual fund (independent of fund domicile) can qualify for the sample as long as that mutual fund is (or has been[125]) registered for distribution in at least one of the considered European core markets.

Type of fund management style

Similar to all previous research works that have been reviewed in chapter 1.2., also models of this thesis are only including actively managed open-ended mutual funds.

Share-class

Consistent with Ferreira et al. (2012) and in order to eliminate multiple observations for one and the same fund strategy, all mutual fund samples are additionally limited to primary-tranches.[126]

---

[124] Chapter 2.2.3. is disclosing insights into the increasing cross-border activity within the European mutual fund market.

[125] Due to a survivorship-free data sample all models are also incorporating funds that already ceased to exist.

[126] Ferreira et al. (2012) p. 1761.

Minimum track record

Due to the predefined time horizon (as explained in chapter 5.1.2.) all included funds must have been active sometime between August 31, 2004 and August 31, 2013. Moreover since observed annual performance figures and fund (net) flow are being contrasted by introducing a time-lag of one year, all funds require a (continuous) minimum track record of at least 24 months.

Legal fund structure

Since the quantitative empirical part of this thesis is aiming to firstly research the flow-performance relationship under the assumption of a cross-border mutual fund competition for a pooled sample of European nationalities, it is only taking into account mutual funds that, based on their legal structure, do easily qualify for cross-border distribution. As it has already been outlined in chapter 2.2.2., UCITS-funds are obtaining a relatively transparent status and can easily be marketed and distributed on a cross-border basis (at least within the European Union). [127] Hence, the sample is moreover limited to only considering mutual funds that, based on Lipper database queries, do possess a UCITS-structure.

Asset class focus

In addition the methodology of the flow-performance relationship research of this thesis is assuming that, when conducting investment decisions, mutual fund investors are only comparing those funds on a relative basis that belong to the exact same asset class (e.g. it is not assumed that a potential investor would directly contrast properties (performance, risk, size, style,...) of an Equity US Income fund with an Equity Global Emerging Market fund – as both investments are engaged in entirely different markets). Since this thesis is emphasizing on highlighting the case for the European mutual fund cross-border market, the author has decided to further limit the sample to mutual funds that, based on Lipper database queries, can be attributed to the "Lipper Global Equity Europe" sub-asset class. According to Lipper, fund strategies are being classified as "Equity Europe", if they are exhibiting a strategic investment exposure to the European stock market as a whole (as opposed to European single-country equity funds (e.g. "Equity Austria")).[128]

---

[127] SEI (2013) online.

[128] Lipper (2008) p.5.

5.1.4. Required data types

Now that the sample focus has been clarified, it is time to turn to the specific kinds of data types this thesis is depending on. In order to be able to empirically answer the research questions and hypotheses raised in chapter 1.3., the later employed quantitative models are primarily relying on the following types of data:

(i) Historical performance figures

Since measuring the relationship between past performance and future net inflows is one of the key-tasks of this thesis, it has to be specified which kinds of past performance are being used as input factors for the empirical models. The author decided upon including three types of performance figures:

Percentage growth:

Annual percentage growth is calculated based on the formula demonstrated in chapter 3.1.2. and has been obtained on a monthly rolling basis for all funds fulfilling the criteria presented in the previous sub-chapter 5.1.3. Since percentage growth is based upon changes in Net Asset Values (NAVs), these values are net of any administrative expenses (management fee and other operating fees) but do not account for front-end-loads (sales commissions) or back-end loads (redemption fees).[129]

Additionally, in order to ensure comparability between accumulating and distributing funds, all performance values are calculated based on the assumption that dividends are invested immediately after occurrence, which is in line with comparable research.[130]

Volatility (standard deviation):

Just as for percentage growth also standard-deviation of all included funds has been calculated based on the formula of 3.1.2.. Data exports have been conducted for annualized standard-deviations[131] on a monthly rolling basis.

---

[129] Mobius (2007) pp. 87-95.

[130] Ferreira et al. (2012) p. 1762.

[131] Monthly standard deviations multiplied by the square root of 12.

Sharpe ratio:

In order to be consistent with the above presented performance-, respectively risk-figures (due to reasons of simplicity henceforth summarized as "performance figures"), also annualized Sharpe ratio exports have been carried out on a monthly rolling basis. Since this thesis is focusing on the behavior of European investors, it is using the 3-month EURIBOR as the relevant risk-free benchmark for all Sharpe Ratio calculations.

General remark regarding the selected performance figures

Please be advised that the focus has not been on selecting those figures with the highest informative value, but to simply include the most common – and therefore most wide-spread measures.

(ii) Historical fund flows

Another centrally essential task for the aims of this thesis is the implementation of historical mutual fund flows. In line with the methodology of all reviewed comparable research (with the exception of Ber et al. (2007)[132]) fund flows are also derived synthetically. In contrast to synthetic fund flow calculations of similar research, the author has decided to base fund flow data upon the methodology of the "Lipper fund flow module", which automatically calculates synthetically derived fund flows for arbitrary time-spans. The major difference between the "Fund flow module" and traditionally employed models is the fact that the methodology of the first one assumes that fund inflows (or outflows) have occurred constantly over the selected time-span, whereas the latter one assumes all fund flows to have taken place in the middle of the respective time-span.

For the detailed formula applied by the "Lipper fund flow module" please consult the subsequent formula.

$$ENS = \frac{f(t_2) - f(t_1) * p_{t_1 t_2}}{\sqrt{p_{t_1 t_2}}}$$

Illustration 12: Methodology of Lipper fund flow module

[132] Ber et al. (2007) have been able to access actual fund flows provided by the German mutual fund association (BVI).

Where:

ENS	Estimated Net Sales (i.e. fund (net) in- or outflows)
t_1	Start Date of Calculation
t_2	End Date of Calculation
$f(t_1)$	Fund Size at t_1
$f(t_2)$	Fund Size at t_2
$p_{t_1 t_2}$	Adjusted Fund Performance from t_1 to t_2(factor form)

(iii) Assets under management (AUM) of fund management companies

For the sake of being able to measure the impact of a fund management company's size on its ability to attract increased (relative) inflows, the author has exported an extensive data set of fund volume data (for all mutual funds that are or have been registered for distribution within at least one European country[133]) for 109 different, monthly valuation dates. Since "Lipper for Investment Management" also provides details on the respective fund management company, a specific fund is related to (in form of master data) the total AUM-value of a fund management company has been achieved by simply aggregating all single-fund volumes up to a fund management company's level (separately for all 109 valuation dates).

[133] A detailed list of all covered European countries is provided in document D in the appendix.

5.2. Data sample

Now that the theoretical details regarding sample derivation as well as herewith associated underlying assumptions, such as the incorporation of an alternative, cross-border based perception of competition between mutual funds, have been discussed in detail, it is time to structurally present some of the major properties and summary statistics of the actually derived sample.

Fund count

Based on the sample limitations of chapter 5.1.3. the employed database (Lipper for Investment Management) provided a total fund list consisting of 1,988 different European equity funds, that do qualify for further processing in the quantitative models for at least one observation date. Due to the fact that the models of this thesis are accounting for a potential survivorship bias (i.e. completely disregarding no longer existing funds) [134], the number of observations is varying for each valuation date – this fluctuation can be a result of fund liquidations, mergers or newly issued funds.

The subsequent chart provides additional details on the development of the number of incorporated fund observations over the selected research horizon (August-2002 – August-2013):

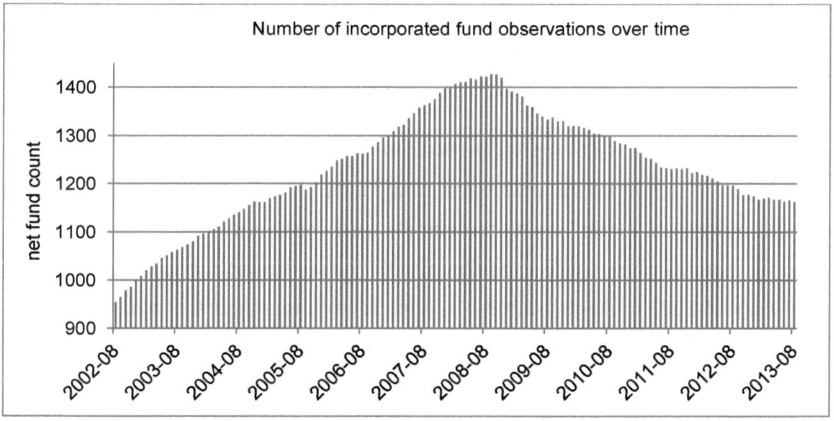

Illustration 13: Development of the number of incorporated sample size over time

[134] CAIA Association (2009) p. 240.

From a total included fund sample of 1,988 funds (retrieved from the Lipper database), only 1,162 funds have been listed as "active" as per August 31, 2013 (final valuation date of all herein applied quantitative models) – which further underscores the necessity of accounting for survivorship-bias. Illustration 13 clearly demonstrates that the global financial crisis of 2008 has obviously marked a significant turning point for the market for European equity funds, as the number of funds has almost been perfectly monotonously decreasing ever since then. When taking a closer look at the subsequently depicted chart, this "paradigm-shift" becomes even more apparent:

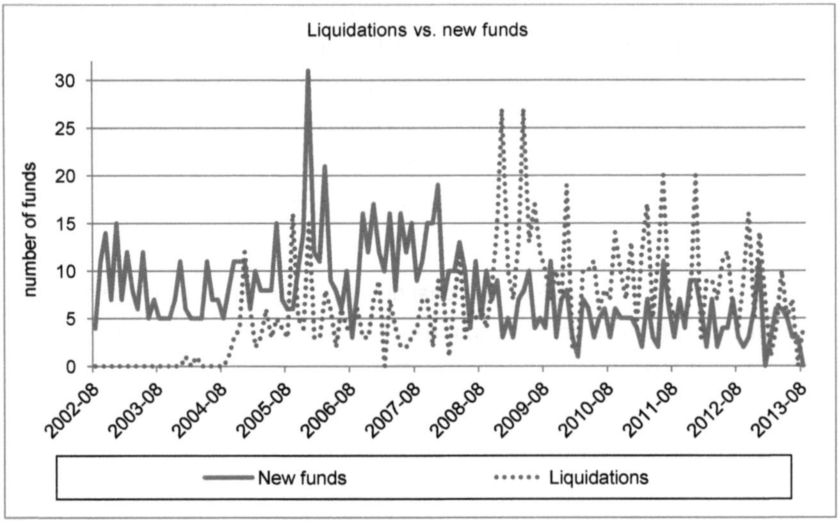

Illustration 14: Comparison: Number of fund liquidations vs. new funds over time

Illustration 14 compares the number of new funds entering the sample (blue line) with the number of funds leaving the sample (red line) on a monthly basis. Cumulating all monthly observations results in 1,032 newly issued funds within the period of August-2002 to August-2008 – in contrast to a total figure of 820 funds leaving the sample within that period. As chapter 5.3.1. will discuss in closer detail, the changing number of observations over time is being accounted for by normalizing regression input values.

Fund (net) flows

Since fund (net) flows constitute one of the most vital input factors for all the later conducted quantitative empirical analyses, it is highly important to also present empirical summary statistics on the development of average relative fund (net) flows of the derived sample. Subsequently displayed Illustration 15 is therefore presenting details on the development of the sample's median, first and third quartile annual relative (fund) flows on a monthly rolling basis for the entire fund (net) flow observation period (August 2004-August 2013):

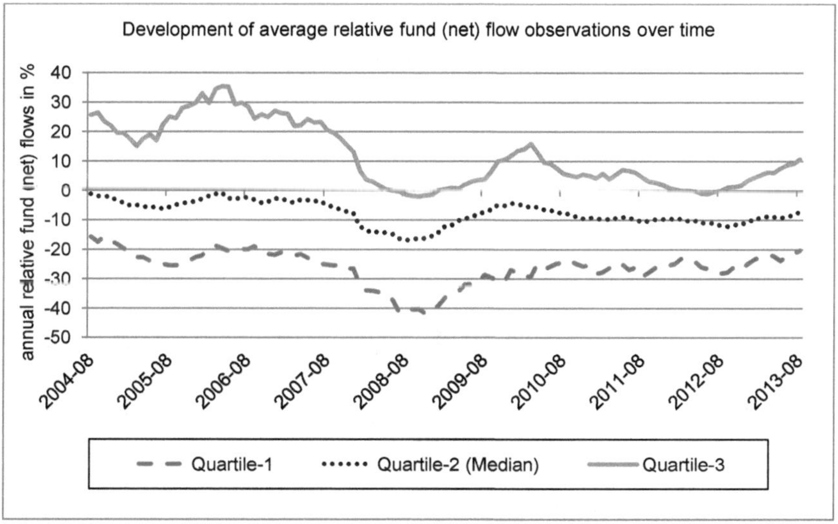

Illustration 15: Development of average relative fund (net) flow observations over time (annual figures, monthly rolling)

Based on the above displayed chart, a further disadvantageous development within the market for Equity Europe mutual funds has become unveiled: Within the observed sample more than 50% (and thus the majority) of all monthly rolling annual relative (fund) net flows have constantly been negative throughout the entire observation period (covering a total of 109 observation dates). Since the average mutual fund of the sample must have really experienced a considerably hard time attracting (net) investments, some of the main implications of this thesis (identifying key-drivers and their influence on the flow-performance relationship) should also be useful for practical purposes as well.

Fund volumes

Since fund volume figures represent yet another important input factor of the upcoming quantitative (regression) models, developments regarding aggregated as well as averaged fund volume observations of the derived sample need to be accounted for within summary statistics. Data collection for fund volumes has been conducted for 109 monthly valuation dates (August 2003 to August 2012). The following chart is providing details on the historical development of (i) first quartile, (ii) second quartile (median), (iii) third quartile fund volume values of all observations.

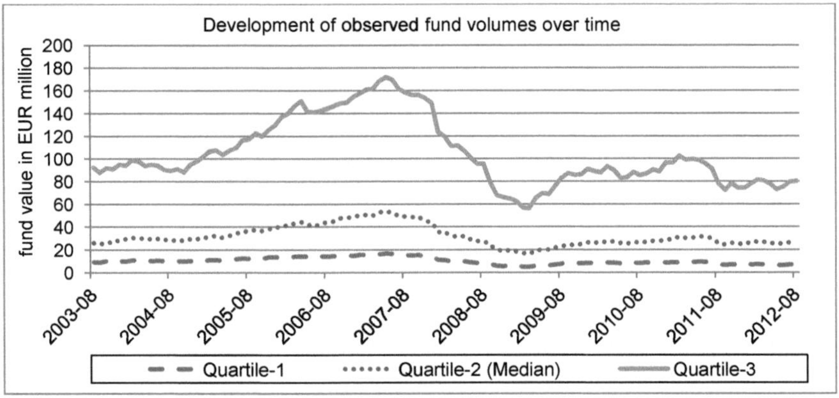

Illustration 16: Development of observed fund volumes over time

5.3. Quantitative methods

This sub-chapter presents the methodology of all quantitative models that are being employed in the upcoming chapter 6 (an interpretation of results is provided in chapter 7). At first general remarks regarding model methodology as well as details regarding data preparation (e.g. handling data inconsistencies or smoothening the impacts of potential outliers) are presented. This is then followed by a detailed step-by-step description of all developed models (correlation and regression models).

5.3.1. General remarks

Since the quantitative models of this thesis are processing an extraordinarily comprehensive empirical data set (see previous sub-chapter 5.2 for detailed summary statistics), a number of potentially harmful obstacles had to be overcome before feeding the models with data. In concrete terms, the following adjustments had to be conducted in order to enable a correct data usage:

(i) Data inconsistencies

The main aim of this thesis is to measure the impact of various mutual fund performance figures (percentage growth, volatility and Sharpe ratio) on subsequently observed fund flows (net in- or out-flows). Thus all empirical quantitative models only incorporate data of mutual funds that are reporting both performance figures as well as fund flows for at least one pair of required observation dates (e.g. 1-Y Sharpe ratio reported on August 31st 2010 and 1-Y fund flows reported on August 31st 2011).

(ii) Removing size-related biases

As previous chapters (see for instance 2.2.3.) have already pointed out clearly, mutual fund sizes are far away from being uniform (not even normally distributed). Due to the potential bias of taking absolute fund flows (in currency terms), the author has decided to take relative values of observed synthetic fund flows instead (directly obtained from the "Lipper for Investment Management" database), which is similar to the methodology of comparable research.[135]

(iii) Smoothening of observations

All included observations (both fund flow values as well as related performance figures) have additionally been protected against outliers by assigning them their relative rank within the remaining peer-group (rather than taking the actually observed values). The basic idea behind transforming observations into ranks is based on the highly competitive character of the mutual fund market landscape. It is assumed that investors compare mutual funds with homogenous objectives and characteristics on an isolated basis. Moreover they then rather focus on comparing the remaining funds based on their relative position (e.g. top-decile/ top-quantile) within the peer-group (which is also supported by the wide-spread phenomenon of fund rankings).[136]

---

[135] E.g. Ferreira et al. (2012) p. 1761. or Ber et al. (2007) p.11.

[136] Comparable to Ber et al. (2007) p. 12.

Additionally when preparing all relevant data samples for regression model input, a time homogenous variable interval is being achieved by normalizing the previously calculated ranks of each data sample on a spectrum from 1 (best observed percentage growth, Sharpe ratio, or relative fund (net) flow value within the sample, respectively highest observed volatility) to 0 (smallest observed value). The applied normalization concept can be denoted as follows:

$$x_{new} = \frac{x - x_{min}}{x_{max} - x_{min}}$$

Illustration 17: Formula for normalization of variables

Please note that, based on the above stated formula, X , $X_{min}$and X_{max}values represent non-normalized rank values that have been generated for each incorporated performance- and fund flow figure prior to normalization. Data normalization is needed in order to increase the robustness of the later presented pooled regression, as the sample size is not being constant over time.

5.3.2. Correlation models

The aim of all herein employed correlation models is to separately measure the relationship between a set of three different performance figures (percentage growth, volatility and Sharpe ratio (constituting the independent variable x)) and lagged relative fund flows (constituting the dependent variable y). Since all processed data values have been transformed into relative ranks, this thesis is making use of Spearman's ρ as a model for measuring rank correlations. In case of sub-samples without ties, the author has applied the simplified Spearman's correlation test which is being presented in the subsequent illustration.[137]

$$\rho = 1 - \frac{6 \sum d_i^2}{n(n^2 - 1)}.$$

Illustration 18: Calculation of Spearman's ρ (in case of no ties)

Please note that within the just depicted formula, d_i^2 represents the squared difference between a (ranked) researched data pair and *n* denotes the number of ob-

[137] Elsevier (n.a.) pp. 385-387.

served data pairs. For the relatively unlikely event that a researched sub-sample is containing ties (e.g. due-to rounding limitations of the Lipper database) the following formula has been employed to measure Spearman's ρ.[138]

$$\rho = \frac{\sum_i (x_i - \bar{x})(y_i - \bar{y})}{\sqrt{\sum_i (x_i - \bar{x})^2 \sum_i (y_i - \bar{y})^2}}.$$

Illustration 19: Calculation of Spearman's ρ (in case of ties)

Correlations coefficients are being calculated separately for the relationships of all three selected, ranked and normalized performance figures (percentage growth, volatility and Sharpe ratio) in *t* and their according ranked and normalized fund flow observations in *t+1*. Additionally Spearman's ρ values are generated on a monthly-rolling basis, thereby leading to an extensive set of 109 different (monthly) observation points for each of the three researched relationships. Hence with the results of the just stated approach, this thesis will be able to firstly[139] display a rolling development of the fund performance-fund flow relationship (measured by Spearman's rank correlation). This feature is considered especially valuable as it can be assumed that the relationship might not be constant over time, but could rather be exposed to specific trends (e.g. a potentially observable increasing risk-awareness of investors after the financial crisis of 2008).[140]

In order to test all collected (rolling) Spearman correlation coefficients for significance, both one- and two-sided t-tests are conducted for all observations at 0.1%-, 1%-, 5%- and 10%-*α* (significance) levels. In case of two-sided tests the null hypothesis that ρ values are not significantly varying from zero is being challenged whereas in the one-sided t-tests the null hypothesis of ρ values depicting a true correlation that is less or equal to zero is being tested.[141] Respective t-values are being calculated based on the following formula (Illustration 20), which employs two degrees of freedom (*n* -2) and where ρ denotes the previously generated Spearman's correlation coefficient.[142]

---

[138] Elsevier (n.a.) pp. 385-387.

[139] To the author's best knowledge.

[140] Elsevier (n.a.) pp. 385-387.

[141] Siegel (2011) pp. 274-276.

[142] Elsevier (n.a.) pp. 385-387.

$$t = \rho \sqrt{\frac{n-2}{1-\rho^2}}$$

Illustration 20: Calculating t-values for hypothesis testing

In case of calculated t-values which are exceeding their respective critical values (taken from the Student's t-distribution) the null hypothesis is being rejected and thus the alternative hypothesis (indicating a significant relation between the incorporated variables (at the relative α levels)) is being accepted.[143]

5.3.3. Regression models

Whereas the just described rolling correlation models are primarily aiming to capture potentially time-specific dynamics and trends in the researched variable-relationships by separately contrasting the correlations within monthly changing sub-samples, the upcoming regression models are designed to quantify the various researched relationships by taking into account the entire sample (i.e. all observations over the whole researched data horizon).

Due to the fact that, nowadays computational power is no longer considered a seriously restricting factor, the author has decided to apply a broader set of different kinds of regression models (with different levels of complexity and expressiveness). The detailed composition of all employed regression models are being presented in the following sub-sections (sorted by complexity). General remarks regarding the model quality and significance tests of the deployed regression models are provided at the end of this sub-chapter.

(i) Bivariate-OLS regression models

In order to get a first feeling for the interrelations within the researched sample (and to already test them for any indications for significance), the author has decided on setting up (straight forward) bivariate linear regression models separately for all three flow-performance figure relationships:

---

[143] Elsevier (n.a.) pp. 385-387.

(a) Bivariate-OLS regression model: Flow-Percentage growth relationship

$$Flow_{t+1} = \alpha + \beta_1 Percentage\ Growth_t + \varepsilon$$

Illustration 21: Bivariate-OLS regression model: Flow-Percentage growth relationship

(b) Bivariate-OLS regression model: Flow-Volatility relationship

$$Flow_{t+1} = \alpha + \beta_1 Volatility_t + \varepsilon$$

Illustration 22: Bivariate-OLS regression model: Flow-Volatility relationship

(c) Bivariate-OLS regression model: Flow-Sharpe ratio relationship

$$Flow_{t+1} = \alpha + \beta_1 Sharpe\ ratio_t + \varepsilon$$

Illustration 23: Bivariate-OLS regression model: Flow-Sharpe ratio relationship

(ii) Piecewise bivariate-OLS regression models

Since the majority of comparable research has concluded that the flow-performance relationship is actually rather depicting a convex than a linear connection, this thesis is also allowing for this particular possibility (non-linearity) by conducting piecewise bivariate linear regressions for each of the three researched flow-performance relationships (flow-percentage growth, flow-volatility, flow-Sharpe ratio). Piecewise regressions are being conducted separately, based on performance-quartiles, thereby generating a set of four different regression slopes for each researched bivariate relationship.

$$Quartile\ 1{:}\ Flow_{t+1} = \alpha + \beta_1 Performance\ Figure_t + \varepsilon$$

$$Quartile\ 2{:}\ Flow_{t+1} = \alpha + \beta_2 Performance\ Figure_t + \varepsilon$$

$$Quartile\ 3{:}\ Flow_{t+1} = \alpha + \beta_3 Performance\ Figure_t + \varepsilon$$

$$Quartile\ 4{:}\ Flow_{t+1} = \alpha + \beta_4 Performance\ Figure_t + \varepsilon$$

Illustration 24: Piecewise bivariate-OLS regression mode

In order to demonstrate possible non-linearity, collected regression slopes for each quartile are eventually being aggregated in ascending order (i.e. β_1 to β_4) and then plotted in one single chart.

(iii) Multivariate OLS-regression models measuring convexity

Similar to previous research works (e.g. Ber et al. (2007)), the author has decided not to only limit convexity tests to piecewise bivariate regressions (see (ii) for more information), but also test for possible convexities within the researched relationships by applying a simplified multivariate model. In contrast to (ii), where convexity was being tested for by applying piecewise regressions (a higher positive coefficient in the upper quartile is an indication of convexity), possible non-linearity is now being accounted for by an alternative approach. The alternative approach is following the suggestions of Barber/Odean/Zheng (2005) and is testing for possible convexity by conducting a pooled regression that is also incorporating the squared performance figure rank of a fund as an independent variable. Based on this approach, any researched relationship is depicting a convex nature whenever the squared term is obtaining a positive regression coefficient.

$$Flow_{t+1} = \alpha + \beta_1 Performance\ Figure_t + \beta_2 Performance\ Figure_t{}^2 + \varepsilon$$

Illustration 25: Multivariate OLS-regression model measuring convexity

(iv) Extended multivariate OLS-regression models

In order to follow the paths of comparable research and to increase explanatory power of the modeled relationships, this thesis is also employing extended multivariate linear-regression models that, besides taking into account (ranked and normalized) performance-figures and their squared values, also incorporate fund age, fund size (similar to related research these figures are only considered by taking their log-values)[144], ranked relative fund flows of the previous year (in order to account for recency bias (see chapter 4.1 for details). In contrast to previous research[145] this thesis is not only accounting for volatility by implementing it as a simple control variable within regression models, but instead puts increased focus on this variable by separately measuring the flow-volatility relationship in discrete multivariate regression models.

---

[144] Ber et al. (2007) p. 14.

[145] E.g. Ber et al. (2007).

The applied extended multivariate OLS-regression models are being calculated separately for all three researched flow-performance figure relationships and can be denoted as follows:

$$Flow_{t+1} = \alpha + \beta_1 Performance\ Figure_t + \beta_2 Performance\ Figure_t{}^2 + \beta_3 (\ln) Fund\ Age_t + \beta_4 (\ln) Fund\ Size_t + \beta_5 Flow\ _t + \varepsilon$$

Illustration 26: Extended multivariate OLS-regression model

Please note that the number of incorporated observations for the above denoted regression model is lower than in (iii) as it is also incorporating fund flows in *t* and thus disregards one full year of observations.

(v) Extended multivariate OLS-regression models measuring impact of total asset manager AUM

For the sake of being able to answer research question 3 and to thus measure the significance, direction and magnitude of the impact of an asset manager's total assets under management (AUM) on the flow-performance relationship, the subsequent multivariate regression model is additionally including normalized AUM figures (from 0 to 1) as explanatory variables. Please note that "Lipper for Investment Management" does not provide total AUM data on each fund management company (i.e. asset manager) and that the number of observations in model (v) is therefore smaller than in (iv).

The alternative multivariate OLS-regression model can thus be denoted as follows:

$$Flow_{t+1} = \alpha + \beta_1 Performance\ Figure_t + \beta_2 Performance\ Figure_t{}^2 + \beta_3 (\ln) Fund\ Age_t + \beta_4 (\ln) Fund\ Size_t + \beta_5 Flow\ _t + \beta_6 AUM_t + \varepsilon$$

Illustration 27: Extended multivariate OLS-regression model measuring total AUM impact

(vi) Model validation and significance testing

For all the just introduced regression models, model quality is being quantified by providing the respective coefficients of determination (R^2-values) as indicator of regression fit. In addition t-test statistics are being conducted for all included explanatory variables at 0.1%, 1%-, 5%- and 10% significance levels.

6. Time series analysis

This chapter constitutes one of the most essential core parts of this thesis as it will step-by-step present the results of all statistical tests that have been conducted based on the quantitative empirical models defined in chapter 5.3.. A detailed interpretation of the collected results in respect of all raised researched questions and hypotheses is then being performed in the subsequent chapter 7.

6.1. Correlation analysis

As it has already been mentioned in chapter 5.3.2. previous contributions in the field of flow-performance analysis have generally researched the flow-performance relationship based on regression models that process a data sample that is pooled over the entire observation period – and thus did not account for potential trends or other structural patterns within the underlying variable relations. Although this thesis will also follow this approach in the later presented regression analyses, it seeks to deliver some insights and indications for potential trends by presenting the following results of monthly rolling rank correlation coefficient tests (based on Spearman's ρ) the following three types of relations:

(i) percentage growth vs. lagged fund (net flows)

(ii) volatility vs. lagged fund (net flows)

(iii) Sharpe ratio vs. lagged fund (net flows)

Each analysis will start off by presenting and commenting on plotted results and will then present details on the statistical significance of the observed correlation coefficients.

Rank correlation: percentage growth vs. lagged fund (net flows)

Rank correlation coefficients (Spearman's ρ) between a mutual fund's empirically observed annual percentage growth-based rank in *t* and a mutual funds annual relative fund (net) flow-based rank in *t+1y* have been generated on a monthly rolling basis for a total of 109 different observation points.

The subsequent chart is presenting the development of generated correlation coefficients for *Percentage growth ~ lagged fund (net flows)* in chronological order:

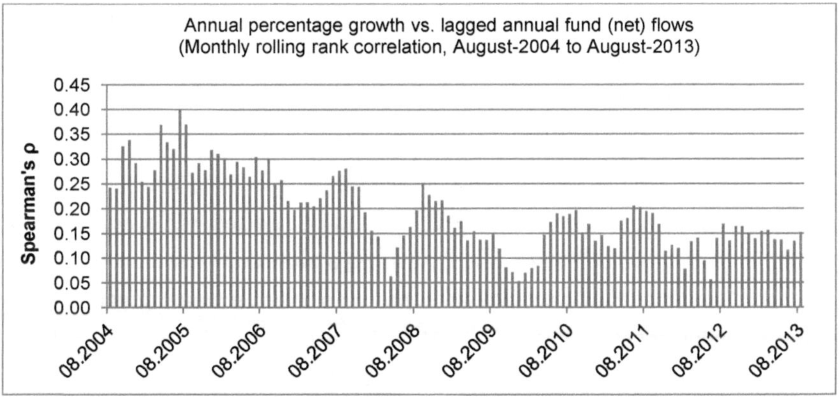

Illustration 28: Monthly rolling rank-correlation: percentage growth vs. lagged fund (net) flows

Above plotted results are clearly suggesting that - within the observed sample - there is a general tendency towards a positive relationship between annual past performance figures (measured by ranked percentage growth) and subsequently observed, ranked relative fund (net) flows. From 109 monthly conducted correlation-tests, not a single valuation-date resulted in a negative correlation-coefficient. However, it is also identifiable that the correlation coefficient of the observed *Percentage growth ~ lagged fund (net flows)* relationship is not static over time and could likely be subject to certain trends or cyclical movements. Volatility of the distribution of coefficients can be further demonstrated by summary statistics: Maximum value of the distribution amounts to a Spearman's ρ of 0.3985 and has been observed in July 2005 (i.e. the underlying sample has been annual percentage growth figures as per July 2004 vs. annual relative fund (net) flows as per July 2005), minimum observed value equals 0.0523 (as per December 2009). Mean of all 109 correlation coefficients is 0.1943 whereas a median ρ of 0.1835 could be detected. Since later presented (bivariate) regression models are researching coefficients for the entire observation period (i.e. conducting a pooled regression) it is expected that regression coefficients will only insignificantly differ[146] from the median observation of the just presented correlation analysis.

[146] Which is primarily due to the fact that, in order to control for varying sample sizes, the pooled regression models will only incorporate ranks on a normalized basis (from 0 to 1).

Collected correlation-coefficients are not only providing indications or tendencies, but are also depicting a high degree of statistical significance – which has been asserted by conducting one- and two- sided t-tests at the following significance levels: 0.1%, 1%, 5% and 10%.

For 91.74% of all observations the null-hypothesis (assuming that the detected relation is depicting a correlation of ≤ 0)[147] could be rejected with a probability of <0.001 under a one-sided t-test, when assuming a two-sided t-distribution (with the null hypothesis that the detected relation has no significant meaning and is just a result of randomness) p-values of <0.001 could be indentified for 90.83% of all 109 observed relationships. In addition, 5.50%, respectively 4.59% (two-sided) of all null hypotheses had to be rejected under a 1% significance level. Subsequently displayed table contains addition information on the distribution of significance levels:

Distribution of significance levels (109 observations)

Significance-levels	one-sided t-test	two-sided t-test
***	91.74%	90.83%
**	5.50%	4.59%
*	2.75%	2.75%
o	0.00%	1.83%
>10%	0.00%	0.00%
Sum	**100.00%**	**100.00%**

Significance codes:
"***" 0.1% level, "**"1% level, "*" 5% level, "o" 10% level.

Table 5: Correlation-test details: percentage growth vs. lagged fund (net) flows

Since the vast majority of null-hypothesis could be rejected at a considerable significance level of less than 0.1%, the just conducted (relatively straight forward) correlation-analysis already provides first evidence on tendencies towards "performance chasing investor behavior" within the researched sample.

Further details on all 109-collected rank correlation coefficients, t-values as well as significance codes are to be found in document A in the appendix.

[147] Siegel (2011) p. 245.

Rank correlation: volatility vs. lagged fund (net flows)

When solely researching the relationship between empirically observed, ranked annualized volatilities (measured by annualized 12 month standard deviation) and lagged, ranked relative fund (net) flows much less tendencies towards a statistically significant relation can be deducted from a purely bivariate correlation-analysis. Just as the subsequent chart presents in detail, coefficients frequently tend to change their direction (from positive to negative, and vice-versa), which suggests the average coefficient to be close to zero.

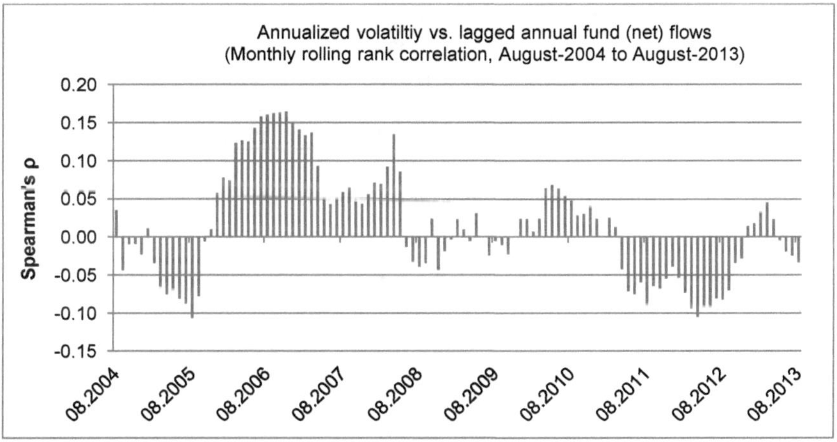

Illustration 29: Monthly rolling rank-correlation: volatility vs. lagged fund (net) flows

However, based on the above presented plot, also the magnitude (as well as direction) of the relation between past volatility and lagged fund (net) flows generally seems to be following certain cyclical-trends (e.g. "risk-on, risk-off "modes) – with the exception of the period between (approximately) August 2008 and August 2010, which does not unveil any specific tendencies on risk attitudes of investors.

Summary statistics on the distribution of generated Spearman's rank coefficients are generally supporting this hypothesis: A minimum coefficient of -0.1061 (as per August 2005) marks the lower bound of the distribution, whereas 0.1644 constitutes the upper boundary. Averaged coefficient values are close to zero: Mean value equals 0.0135 and the median amounts to 0.0098.

Compared to the results of the previously analyzed *Percentage growth ~ lagged fund (net flows)* relationship, generated coefficients are considerably less statistically significant: Only 14.68% of all 109 observations achieved a p-value of <0.001 under a one-sided t-test (13.76% under a two-sided t-distribution). In 41.28% of all cases the null-hypothesis had to be accepted (two-sided: 52.29%). Table 6 is presenting combined test-results for all 109 valuation dates.

Distribution of significance levels (109 observations)

Significance-levels	one-sided t-test	two-sided t-test
***	14.68%	13.76%
**	15.60%	9.17%
*	17.43%	18.35%
o	11.01%	6.42%
>10%	41.28%	52.29%
Sum	**100.00%**	**100.00%**

Significance codes:
"***" 0.1% level, "**"1% level, "*" 5% level., "o" 10% level.

Table 6: Correlation-test details: Volatility vs. lagged fund (net) flows

Separate test statistics for all 109 coefficients are provided in document B in the appendix.

Rank correlation: Sharpe ratio vs. lagged fund (net flows)

Whereas both previously researched key-figures (percentage growth and volatility) can be characterized by their unidirectional focus (pure performance vs. pure risk[148]), Sharpe ratio presents the only multidirectional (since risk-adjusted) performance figure that is closely being researched within the quantitative models of this thesis. A look at the magnitude as well as direction of the subsequently plotted coefficient values strongly reminds one of the previously presented *Percentage growth ~ lagged fund (net flows)* relationship (Illustration 28) – which, since percentage growth is one important input factor of the Sharpe ratio, is actually not that surprising.

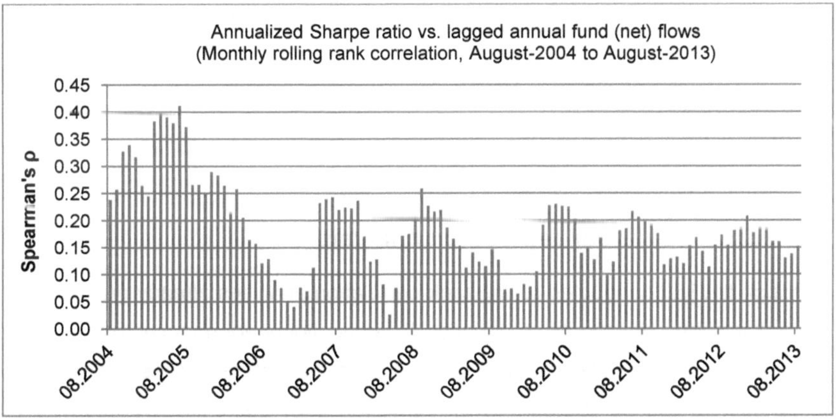

Illustration 30: Monthly rolling rank-correlation: Sharpe ratio vs. lagged fund (net) flows

Important location parameters of the above distribution are as follows: lower bound: at 0.0261 (as per April 2008), upper bound at 0.4116 (as per July 2005), mean at 0.1833 and median at 0.1748. Surprisingly, both mean and median values are slightly below the comparable values of the *Percentage growth ~ lagged fund (net flows)* distribution, thus indicating that investors might tend to rather base their decisions on a pure performance and not-risk adjusted performance base. This suggestion is also marginally supported by the results of the significance tests for the 109 (monthly) researched *Sharpe ratio ~ lagged fund (net flows)* relations. Similar to the results of *Percentage growth ~ lagged fund (net flows)* the vast ma-

[148] However, by means of ordinary volatility calculation also upside-deviations are considered „risk".

jority of null hypotheses could be rejected at a highly significant p-value of <0.001 (87.16% both one- and two-sided). For 7.34%, respectively 3.67% (two-sided) of all cases null hypotheses were rejected at a 1% significance level. Only for 1.83% (one-sided) and 2.75% (two-sided) of researched relationships, the null hypothesis had to be accepted. Please see table 7 for combined results of significance tests:

Distribution of significance levels (109 observations)

Significance-levels	one-sided t-test	two-sided t-test
***	87.16%	87.16%
**	7.34%	3.67%
*	2.75%	6.42%
o	0.92%	0.00%
>10%	1.83%	2.75%
Sum	**100.00%**	**100.00%**

Significance codes:
"***" 0.1% level, "**"1% level, "*" 5% level., "o" 10% level.

Table 7: Correlation-test details: Sharpe ratio vs. lagged fund (net) flows

Detailed correlation-test results as well as significance codes for all 109 observation points are provided in document C in the appendix.

6.2. Bivariate linear regression analysis

Although the just conducted rolling rank-correlation analyses already provided significant insights into the three focuses bivariate flow-performance relationships, this subchapter will deliver additional details on the nature of these relations by performing (i) pooled bivariate OLS-regression over the entire sample and (ii) piecewise (segmented) bivariate OLS-regressions that will search for potential hints for potential non-linearity in the underlying relationships (ideally in the form of convexity). Please note that, for the sake of addressing the need of harmonizing sub-samples with different numbers of observations, all pooled regression models are processing performance and flow ranks on a normalized basis (from 0 to 1).

(i) Pooled bivariate OLS-regressions

For the sake of measuring static relationship coefficients for the entire observation period, all variables of all 109 distinct (monthly rolling) sub-samples have been normalized and subsequently been merged in to one main data sample. Thus all upcoming regression models have been able to profit from a comprehensive data sample of 114,817 observations.

Just like in the correlation analyses, bivariate OLS-regressions have been calculated separately for (i) flow-percentage growth, (ii) flow-volatility as well as (iii) flow-Sharpe ratio relationships. Consistent with previous calculations, performance-ranks (respectively risk-ranks) have been contrasted to fund (net) flows that have been observed one year later (i.e. applying a time-lag of one-year). Regression results as well as significance codes for all three relations are being jointly displayed in the subsequent table:

Results of pooled bivariate OLS-regressions

	(i) flow~percentage growth	(ii) flow~volatility	(iii) flow~Sharpe ratio
Intercept	0.406792 ***	0.493866 ***	0.411543 ***
Performance figure	0.186417 ***	0.012268 ***	0.176914 ***
R^2	0.0348	0.0002	0.0313
No. of observations	111,487	111,487	111,487

Significance codes: "****" 0.1% level, "***"1% level, "*" 5% level., "o" 10% level.

Table 8: Combined results of pooled bivariate OLS-regressions

Not surprisingly regression coefficients for all three researched relationships do not dramatically differ from the average (median, respectively arithmetic mean) values detected in the monthly-rolling correlation analyses (see chapter 6.1 for details). Also the high statistical significance of (i) percentage growth and (iii) Sharpe ratio could have already been anticipated based on the highly indicative significance tests of the rolling correlation coefficients. However, the fact that (ii) *flow~volatility* is also depicting such a statistically highly significant (p-value <0.001) relationship, would not have been assumed based on the largely less significant (one-and two-sided t-test based) results that have been observed for the 109 monthly correlation coefficient estimates Having said that, it is still highly doubtful that solely considering the *flow~volatility* coefficient of 0.0122 on its own, is having any other serious meaning or implication than statistical significance (e.g. economic significance).

In order to step on step deeper into the dynamics of the three researched bivariate relationships, the upcoming piecewise OLS-regression will disclose details on how each regression coefficient behaves at different performance levels.

(ii) Segmented bivariate OLS-regressions

As chapter 5.3.3. has outlined in detail, piecewise bivariate OLS-regression are being performed for each of the three flow~performance relationships individually. In order to detect potential non-linearity within a relationship, each observed performance-figure sample is grouped into performance-quartiles and is then being contrasted with its according lagged fund (net) flows observations. Thus each piecewise regression essentially comprises four individual OLS-regressions whose slopes are subsequently being compared and plotted into one segmented regression line (in order to better illustrate a potential non-linear behavior).

(i) flow~percentage growth

The following table provides results on the slope (as well as its statistical significance) for all four percentage growth based quartiles:

(i) piecewise –regression: flow~percentage growth

Quartile-1	0.161409***
Quartile-2	0.157506***
Quartile-3	0.12667***
Quartile-4	0.42122***

Significance codes: "***" 0.1% level, "**"1% level, "*" 5% level, "o" 10% level.

Table 9: Coefficients of bivariate OLS-regression: flow~percentage growth

Similar to already mentioned previous research works, also this thesis is detecting indications for a convex relationship between past performance (percentage growth) and lagged relative fund (net) flows. Based on this simplified (bivariate) model, top-quartile mutual funds of the researched sample are 2.61 times more sensitive towards fund (net) flows than bottom-quartile funds.

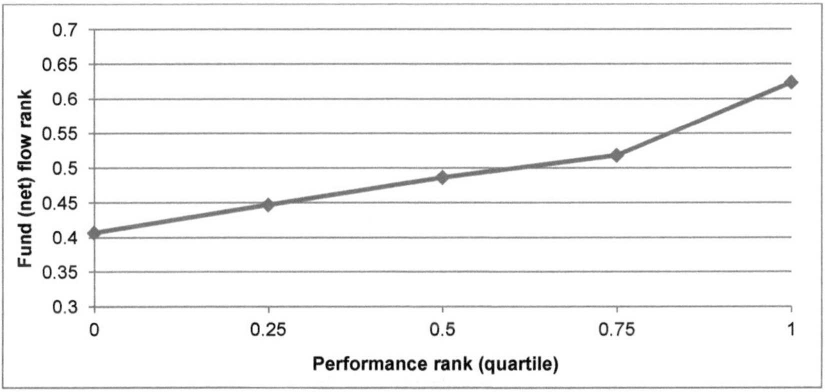

Illustration 31: Connected slopes of piecewise flow~percentage growth regression

Illustration 31 has, step by step, connected the slopes of all above stated segmented (individual) regressions, in order to demonstrate the considerable increase of the regression coefficient in the top-quartile. The statistical significance of this potentially detected convex-relation is being tested within a later presented multivariate OLS-regression that will account for convexity by also incorporating the squared performance as explanatory variable.

(ii) flow~volatility

Piecewise regressions for the first three volatility quartiles are not disclosing any worth mentioning tendencies or sensitivities - moreover they are all not depicting any statistically significance (p-values above 10%-threshold).

(ii) piecewise –regression: flow~volatility

Quartile-1	0.0160
Quartile-2	-0.0097
Quartile-3	0.0152
Quartile-4	-0.14087***

Significance codes: "****" 0.1% level, "***"1% level, "*" 5% level., "o" 10% level.

Table 10: Coefficients of bivariate OLS-regression: flow~volatility

Interestingly however, investors seem to obtain a relatively abrupt, negative, and statistically significant sensitivity towards mutual funds with a top-quartile volatility (i.e. mutual funds with the highest 25% volatility observations). Table 10 depicts the exact slopes of each volatility-quartile whereas Illustration 32 combines the collected slopes graphically.

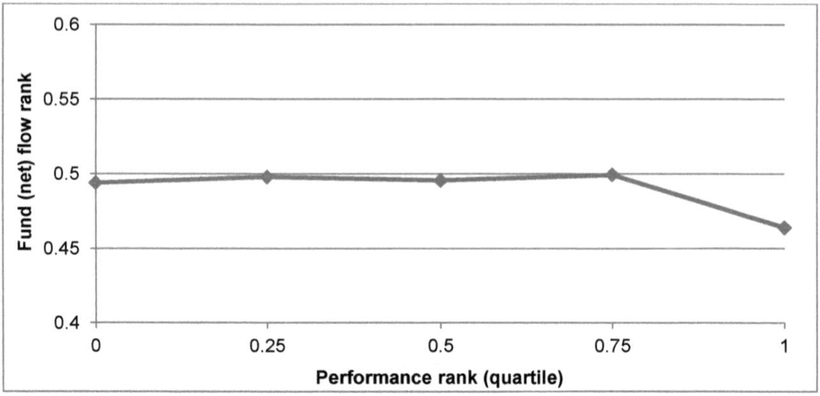

Illustration 32: Connected slopes of piecewise flow~volatility regression

(iii) flow~Sharpe ratio

As it has already been documented within the previously conducted analyses (e.g. rolling correlation-analyses performed in chapter 5.3.2.), the relationships between *flow~percentage growth* and *flow~Sharpe ratio* are demonstrating noticeable co-movements. However, when comparing the results of both piecewise regressions, slight differences regarding the sensitivity at the lower and upper-bounds (i.e. bottom- and top-quartile) become apparent:

(iii) piecewise –regression: flow~Sharpe ratio

Quartile-1	0.271154***
Quartile-2	0.152756***
Quartile-3	0.13073***
Quartile-4	0.39142***

Significance codes: "****" 0.1% level, "***"1% level, "*" 5% level., "o" 10% level.

Table 11: Coefficients of bivariate OLS-regression: flow~Sharpe ratio

As the above displayed table demonstrates, both Quartile-1 and Quartile-4 are possessing the strongest sensitivities (Quartile-1 being 1.78-2.07 times more sensitive than middle-segments, and Quartile-4 even 2.56-3.00 times more sensitive), whereas in the case of *flow~percentage growth* only the top-quartile depicted a significantly increased slope.

The subsequent chart is presenting in the collected segment slopes for the *flow~Sharpe ratio* relationship graphically:

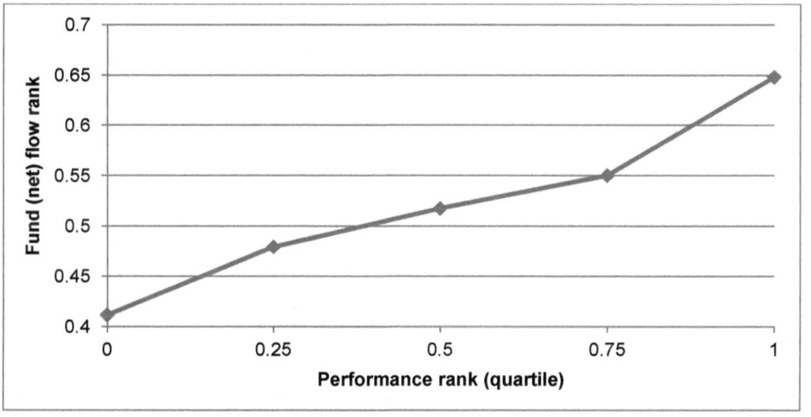

Illustration 33: Connected slopes of piecewise flow~Sharpe ratio regression

6.3. Multivariate linear regression analysis

Based on the methodology of Barber et al. (2005) as well as Ber et al. (2007), a potential convexity in researched flow-performance relationships can additionally be tested for by including the squared performance rank as explanatory variable in a multivariate model. The following table summarizes calculated regression results for a set of three relatively simple multivariate models, where each of them is aiming to explain flows by observed performance ranks and squared performance ranks:

Multivariate OLS-regression models measuring convexity

	(i) flow~percentage growth	(ii) flow~volatility	(iii) flow~Sharpe-ratio
Intercept	0.426398***	0.484946***	0.429229***
Performance figure	0.068664***	0.065837***	0.070699***
Performance figure²	0.117752***	-0.053568***	0.106214***
R^2	0.0357	0.0003	0.0321
No. of observations	111,487	111,487	111,487

Significance codes: "***" 0.1% level, "**"1% level, "*" 5% level., "o" 10% level.

Table 12: Results of multivariate OLS-regression models measuring convexity

According to previous research methodologies, convexity is being identified, if the squared performance ranks is depicting a statistically significant and positive regression coefficient. Since this is the case for *flow~percentage growth* and *flow~Sharpe ratio* the results of the just demonstrated multivariate models are strongly supporting the findings of the previously conducted segmented bivariate models – where indications for potential convexity could have been identified. Moreover, also the statistically significant (negative) regression coefficient of squared volatility ranks is in line with the findings of the segmented bivariate regression approach.

In order to account for the potentially significant influence of additional explanatory, respectively control-variables (and to challenge the findings that have been identified based on previously performed bivariate tests), the following, more-complex multivariate regressions have additionally been conducted, and led to the following results:

In the below presented multivariate OLS-regressions, each of the three flow~ relationships has been separately examined by additionally accounting for a fund's squared performance rank, age and fund size (taken as logarithmic values) in *t* as well as ranked relative fund (net) flows in *t*. Please note that the number of observations is lower for the subsequent analyses as they are including previous year's fund flows and thus are dismissing one set of observation-periods.

Extended multivariate OLS-regression models

	(i) flow~percentage growth	(ii) flow~volatility	(iii) flow~Sharpe ratio
Intercept	0.3027430***	0.3183474***	0.3028196***
Performance figure	0.0545156***	0.0865139***	0.0654021***
Performance figure²	0.0719946***	-0.0730491***	0.0510087***
Fund age in *t* *(ln)*	-0.0049424***	-0.0062977***	-0.0048765***
Fund volume in *t* (ln)	-0.0027846***	-0.0006769***	-0.0029932***
Relative flows in *t*	0.2940778***	0.3157771***	0.2978192***
R²	0.1086	0.0932	0.1060
No. of observations	93,116	93,116	93,116

Significance codes: "***" 0.1% level, "**"1% level, "*" 5% level., "o" 10% level.

Table 13: Results of extended multivariate OLS-regression models

Results of the above stated multivariate models are not harming the key-findings that have been deducted from the previously performed (more simple) models: *flow~percentage growth* and *flow~Sharpe ratio* are still depicting a statistically positive as well as convex relation (due to the positive and significant impact of the squared ranks). Additional control variables age and volume are also demonstrating a statistically significant (negative) impact, however, based on coefficient values being considerably close to zero, a economic significance is highly questioned. Most remarkably, the inclusion of previous-year fund flows as explanatory variable (ranked and normalized) is significantly enhancing each model's fit (with R^2 ranging from 9.32% (flow~volatility) to 10.86% (flow~percentage growth) – now being comparable to the model quality of comparable previous works)[149]. The highly significant and positive coefficient for this control variable is supporting the hypothesis that the herein researched sample might also be affected by the well-documented "recency bias" (see chapter 4.1).

Moreover also the detected statistically significant (slightly) negative impacts of fund age (as discussed in chapter 3.3.) and fund size are consistent with the findings of comparable research studies.[150]

In order to measure the impact of an asset manager's total AUM on the flow-performance relationship, the following multivariate model is additionally including normalized total AUM figures for each incorporated fund. Please note that, due to the fact that "Lipper for Investment Management" does not provide total AUM data for each fund of the sample (or to be specific: information on the according fund management company's total AUM data), the number of observations is smaller than in the previous model (93,116 observations vs. 87,715).

Extended multivariate OLS-regression models measuring total AUM impact

	(i) flow~percentage growth	(ii) flow~volatility	(iii) flow~Sharpe ratio
Intercept	0.3021408***	0.3165020***	0.3030880***
Performance figure	0.0654556***	0.0920713***	0.0790037***
Performance figure²	0.0648525***	-0.0765799***	0.0400868**
Fund age in *t (ln)*	-0.0031914*	-0.0044104**	-0.0032685*
Fund volume in *t* (ln)	-0.0028236***	-0.0007819	-0.0029584***
Relative flows in *t*	0.2934250***	0.3161902***	0.2975768***
Total AUM in *t*	-0.0065568 o	-0.0032865	-0.0080884*
R^2	0.1095	0.09328	0.1065
No. of observations	87,715	87,715	87,715

Significance codes: "***" 0.1% level, "**"1% level, "*" 5% level., "o" 10% level.

Table 14: Results of extended multivariate OLS-regression model measuring total AUM impact

[149] Depending on the respective model type, Ber et al. (2007) achieved R^2 values ranging from 9.92% to 10.20%. Ferreira et al. (2012) employed less explanatory flow-performance models with R^2 ranging from 6.3% to 9.2%.

[150] E.g. Ferreira et al. (2012) p. 1765. or Ber et al. (2007) p. 32.

When looking at the presented model outputs (Table 14) it can be deduced that – within the observed sample (European equity funds following a UCITS-structure) – the relative size of an asset manager (measured by normalized total AUM) is, if at all, only very moderately impacting the flow-performance relationship. Most interestingly, instead of what has been hypothesized, the detected (moderate) influences of total AUM figures are tending towards depicting a negative direction. In case of *flow~percentage growth* a slightly negative impact of total AUM is assessed to be significant at a 10% level. For *flow~volatility* no p-values ≤,10% could be observed, whereas for relationship (iii) *flow~Sharpe ratio* a slightly negative impact of total AUM figures is being significant at a 5% level. The just described less significant explanatory power of an asset management company's total AUM as well as the observed negative tendency of this input variable is inconsistent with the findings of Ber et al. (2007). Within their study on equity funds with German domicile, Ber et al. (2007) were detecting a slightly positive but statistically highly significant impact of fund management company size on their developed flow-performance models.[151]

Regarding the statistical significance, magnitude and direction of the influence of the respective incorporated performance figures (percentage growth, volatility, Sharpe ratio) on the flow-performance models, the reduced sample size (87,715 observations) is not demonstrating a harmful impact. For each of three models p-values remain highly significant (≤0.1%). However, reduced sample size is affecting the statistical significance of the control variables "fund age" (for all three models) and "fund volume" (only for *flow~volatility*).

[151] Ber et al. (2007) p. 33.

7. Empiric evidence

Now that all results of the quantitative empirical models have been presented (see chapter 6 for details), the following part will structurally answer all raised research questions according to the just collected empirical results.

7.1. Research question & hypothesis 1

With regards to the question, whether the key-findings of previous flow-performance research works can also be detected when applying an alternative methodology for sample derivation (with a different underlying perception of how mutual funds are competing against each other for investor inflows), the proposed hypotheses 1(hypothesizing that results will not dramatically vary from comparable previous research methodologies) is largely being supported based on the empirical findings presented in chapter 6. The two main findings of (acknowledged) flow-performance research works (i.e. (i) a significant positive relation between past performance figures and lagged fund (net) flows as well as (ii) tendencies towards a convex form of such relationships) could also be detected for the researched sample of this thesis (which has been derived based on an – so far - unusual methodology). Research question & hypothesis 1.1 and Research question & hypothesis 1.2 are commenting on the herewith related findings in closer detail.

7.1.1. Research question & hypothesis 1.1

Monthly-rolling correlation models for both, *flow~percentage growth* and *flow~Sharpe ratio* relationships, have been able to largely identify highly significant (rank) correlations for both bivariate relations (based on two-sided t-tests). Moreover, based on the findings of one-sided t-tests, the observed rolling correlation coefficients for these two relations are generally not only significantly different from zero, but in fact do also depict a highly significant positive correlation (i.e. true correlation being >0). In case of the *flow~volatility* relationship, results from the rank-correlation tests were not as indicative (null hypothesis had to be rejected in more than 50% of all 109 researched cases (when assuming a 10%-minimum significance level). However, the less significant *flow~volatility* relationship is not really surprising as volatility as a stand-alone variable only possesses highly limited informative value.

Results of the conducted ordinary, bivariate OLS-regression models (that incorporated the entire sample (via pooling of observations)) as well as the collected output of the applied set of more complex multivariate OLS-regression models are also strongly supporting hypothesis 1.1. Within each of the models, the respective performance figures have demonstrated a statistically highly significant (p-values <0.1%) and positive influence on the underlying flow-performance relationship.

7.1.2. Research question & hypothesis 1.2

Regarding the estimated form (non-linearity) of the researched flow-performance relationships, the piecewise OLS-regressions (segmentation based on performance quartile) of chapter 6.2. delivered first, concrete hints on non-linearity: *flow~percentage growth* and *flow~Sharpe ratio* were achieving stronger regression coefficients in the upper quartiles than in the bottom quartiles – which can be interpreted as an indication of convexity within these relationships. In case of *flow~volatility* a strong inverse (negative) slope could be detected for the highest quartile.

Non-linearity has additionally been tested for within multivariate models (by also including the squared performance figure rank as an explanatory variable) and generally supported the tendencies that have been detected within the (comparably simplified) piecewise bivariate OLS-regressions. Within *flow~percentage growth* and *flow~Sharpe ratio* the squared performance figure rank has been able to achieve a highly significant and positive regression coefficient – which based on the methodology of Ber et al. (2007) is constituting further evidence for a convex flow-performance relationship. For *flow~volatility* the squared rank has obtained highly significant negative coefficients – thus also backing the findings of the segmented regressions and indicating that investors are especially sensitive towards particularly large fund volatilities.

With the exception of *flow~volatility,* Hypothesis 1.2 is thus also strongly supported by the empirical findings of this thesis.

7.2. Research question & hypothesis 2

The graphical presentation of an extensive set of calculated rolling rank correlation coefficients for each of the three (bivariate) flow-performance models (plotted within the analyses of chapter 6.1) is providing insights into the historical development of the magnitude and direction of each relationship. In case of *flow~percentage growth* and *flow~Sharpe ratio* correlation coefficients remained positive throughout the entire observation period – and – for the vast majority[152] of rolling periods - were additionally also demonstrating a statistically highly significant meaning. Even though significance and direction of these two relations remained rather stable throughout the observation period, the graphical demonstration as well as an (superficial) analysis of location parameters (especially minimum and maximum values) is providing hints on possible trends within the underlying relationships. A detailed analysis of the statistical significance of such potential trends could become subject of closer research by future studies.

In case of *flow~volatility* the historical development of direction and magnitude of rolling correlation coefficients is depicting a highly unstable character – with coefficients ranging from +0.1644 to -0.1061. Moreover, when interpreting the plotted historical coefficient values certain hints for patterns regarding periods with increased/decreased risk-awareness are being identifiable. As it has been discussed in 7.1.1. the significance of the observed coefficient has been highly limited compared to *flow~percentage growth* and *flow~Sharpe ratio.*

Summing up, empirical findings of the conducted rolling correlation models are generally providing limited but useful hints for potential trends in coefficient magnitude and direction (in case of *flow~volatility)* and thus are supporting hypothesis 2.

7.3. Research question & hypothesis 3

The impact of a fund management company's market presence and marketing power has been tried to be assessed by using a fund management's total AUM figure as a proxy. However, the implementation of (normalized) total AUM figures in the extended multivariate OLS-regression models were not supporting hypothe-

---

[152] p-values <0.1% (both one- and two-sided) for more than 90% of all rolling observations in case of *flow~percentage growth,* and for more than 87% in case of *flow~Sharpe ratio.*

sis 3. Although only with very limited statistical significance (no statistical significance for *flow~volatility,* 10% significance for *flow~percentage growth,* 5% significance *for flow~Sharpe ratio*), total AUM generally exerted a slightly negative influence on the attraction of lagged fund (net) flows. Thus based on this finding, mutual funds of smaller fund management companies (measured by total AUM) tend to attract new fund (net) flows more easily than mutual funds of bigger asset management companies – every other parameters being equal. As a consequence hypothesis 3 has to be rejected.

The detected tendencies towards a negative influence of total AUM on flow-performance relationships is inconsistent with the findings of a comparable empirical research work of Ber et al. (2007). A possible explanation for the contradictory findings could be the fact that Ber et al. (2007) have been examining flow-performance relationships for a broader set of asset classes, whereas this thesis has only been including mutual funds that are being classified as “Equity Europe”.

Conclusion

The opening part of this thesis has performed a detailed review of the most relevant, previous academic contributions in the field of mutual fund flow-performance relationship research and especially focused on working out potential shortcomings regarding research and model methodologies. It concluded that, comparable research projects have generally focused on highlighting the flow-performance relationship for just one fund domicile, thereby automatically limiting the perception of how mutual funds compete against each other.

Chapter 2 provided comprehensive insights into the historical development as well as the current state of competition within European mutual fund industry and worked out that, due to the increased cross-border activity within the European mutual fund industry (e.g. as a result of UCITS-regulations), above mentioned research methodologies might not be applicable to such an open market. This further supported the unconventional flow-performance research methodology of this thesis – which, in contrast to comparable research, is not focusing on highlighting the flow-performance relationship for funds of just one specific domicile, but instead is researching flow-performance dynamics for an extensive cross-border market (entire European market) on the example of an empirical set of European equity funds (UCITS). Sample derivation has completely been disregarding a fund's domicile and solely focused on a fund's potential availability (i.e. sales registration) within the focus region.

The subsequent chapters 3 to 4 then provided some essential background information on the most important input factors and driving factors of flow-performance dynamics. Chapter 3 delivered a critical review of commonly employed (mutual fund) performance and risk measurement methods and (based on the results of a literature meta-analysis) came to the conclusion that there are hardly any proofs for persistency of mutual fund (out-) performance. Since findings of comparable research have generally been identifying significant irrationalities (e.g. detection of significant positive and convex relations) within flow-performance relationships, chapter 4 has focused on assessing such illogical investor decisions from a behavioral finance point of view and worked out that the flow-performance relationship is significantly being affected by "recency bias" (explaining why investors chase (non-persistent) past performance), “disposition effect” (explaining convexity) as well as “status quo bias” (explaining why investors buy the same fund year by year).

Chapters 5 marked the start of the actual (autonomously conducted) quantitative empirical part of this thesis and delivered an in-depth description of sample derivation as well as architecture and logic behind all employed statistical models. The detailed results of all performed statistical tests were structurally presented in chapter 6, whereas chapter 7 condensed the empirical findings by delivering explicit answers for all raised researched questions.

Based on a broad set of statistical tests (rolling Spearman’s rank-correlation tests, (piecewise-) bivariate and multivariate OLS-regression models) this thesis has been able to deliver empirical evidence that the main findings of previous flow-performance research (focusing on solely one fund domicile) also remain valid when the underlying methodologies are being applied to a broad cross-border sample of European equity funds (UCITS-structure). In more detail the quantitative models of this research project have been assessing a highly significant positive relation between past performance (in from of percentage growth and Sharpe-ratio) and lagged fund flows – indicating that investors of the observed sample are demonstrating a certain kind of performance chasing behavior. Moreover, results of segmented bivariate and multivariate OLS-regressions ascertained these relations to be of a non-linear nature – implying that investors react to out- or under-performance with different sensitivity magnitudes.

An extensive set of monthly rolling rank correlation tests disclosed insights into the historical development of each researched flow-performance relation and detected possible hints for potential trends and structural patterns within these variables. A closer study of the time-wise stability of flow-performance relationships could become subject of future research projects.

The implementation of total assets under management of a mutual fund’s fund management company within multivariate models tried to assess the impact of a company’s market presence on its ability to attract flows. However, inconsistent with findings of comparable research methodology (Ber et al. (2007)) this thesis has not been able to proof a significant positive influence of this particular factor.

Bibliography

AXA (2013): Mutual Funds: Understanding The Key Concepts, retrieved from http://www.axa-equitable.com/investments/mutual-funds/key-concepts.html, accessed September 30, 2013

Baird's Advisory Services Research (2011): The (Un) Realiability of Past Performance, Milwaukee: Robert W. Baird & Co. Incorporated, retrieved from http://www.rwbaird.com/bolimages/Media/PDF/Whitepapers/Un-Reliability-Past-Performance.pdf, accessed September 13, 2013

Baker, H. K. / Nofsinger J. R. (2010): Behavioral Finance: Investors, Corporations, and Markets, Hoboken: John Wiley & Sons

Barber, B. M. / Odean T. / Zheng L. (2005): Out of Sight, Out of Mind: The Effects of expenses on Mutual Fund Flows, retrieved from http://faculty.haas.berkeley.edu/odean/Papers%20current%20versions/Out%20of%20Signt.pdf, accessed October 20, 2013

Ber S. / Kempf, A. / Ruenzi, S. (2007): Determinanten der Mittelzuflüsse bei deutschen Aktienfonds, retrieved from http://www.fbv.kit.edu/symposium/10th/papers/Ber_Kempf_Ruenzi%20-%20Determinanten%20der%20Mittelzufluesse%20bei%20deutschen%20Aktienfonds.pdf, accessed October 10, 2013.

Brandimarte, P. (2003): Numerical Methods in Finance: A MATLAB-Based Introduction, New York City: John Wiley & Sons

CAIA Association (2009): An Introduction to Core Topics in Alternative Investments, Hoboken: John Wiley & Sons

CACEIS (2011): Cross-border distribution of UCITS, Luxembourg: CACEIS Investor Services, retrieved from http://www.caceis.com/fileadmin/pdf/reference_papers_en/cross-border-distribution-ucits-v2.pdf, accessed September 15, 2013

Carhart, M. M. (1997): On Persistence in Mutual Fund Performance, in: Journal of Finance, vol. 52., no. 1, pp. 57-82., retrieved from http://www.jstor.org/discover/10.2307/2329556?uid=3737528&uid=2129&uid=2&uid=70&uid=4&sid=21102772130611, accessed September 30, 2013

Chen, J. / Hong, H. / Huang, M. / Kubik, J. (2004): Does Fund Size Erode Mutual Fund Performance? The Role of Liquidity and Organization, in: American Economic Review, vol. 94, no. 5, pp. 1276-1302, retrieved from http://papers.ssrn.com/sol3/papers.cfm?abstract_id=372721, accessed January 31, 2013

Chevalier, J. / Ellison, G. (1997): Risk Taking by Mutual Funds as a Response to Incentives, in: Journal of Political Economy, vol. 105, no. 6, pp. 1167-1200

Ciccotello, C. (2009): Mutual Fund Regulation and Issues, in: Mutual Funds: Portfolio Structures, Analysis, Management and Stewardship, Hoboken: John Wiley & Sons

EFAMA a, (2013): European Monthly Industry Fact Sheet, Brussels: European Fund and Asset Management Association, retrieved from http://www.efama.org/statistics/SitePages/European%20Monthly%20Industry%20Fact%20Sheet.aspx, accessed September 7, 2013

EFAMA b, (2013): About EFAMA, Brussels: European Fund and Asset Management Association, retrieved from http://www.efama.org/about/SitePages/Home.aspx, accessed September 7, 2013

EFAMA c, (2013): International Statistical Release Q1/2013, Brussels: European Fund and Asset Management Association retrieved from http:/www.efama.org/Publications/Statistics/International/Quarterly%20%20International/130702_International%20Statistical%20Release%202013%20Q1.pdf, accessed September 7, 2013

Essvale Corporation Limited (2007): Business Knowledge for IT in Investment Management: The Complete Handbook, London: Essvale Corporation Limited

Fiduciary News (2013): Why 401k Investors Chase Performance – and How to Prevent It, in: Fiduciary News, retrieved from http://fiduciarynews.com/2013/03/why-401k-investors-chase-performance-and-how-to-prevent-it/, accessed November 10, 2013

Ferreira, M. A. / Keswani, A. / Miguel, A. F. / Ramos, S. B (2012): The flow-performance relationship around the world, in: Journal of Banking & Finance, vol. 36, pp. 1759-1780, retrieved from http://www.cass.city.ac.uk/__data/assets/pdf_file/0015/125610/Flow-performance-relationship-around-the-world.pdf, accessed October 15, 2013

FINRA (2013): Mutual Funds, Washington D.C.: Financial Industry Regulatory Authority, retrieved from http://www.finra.org/Investors/SmartInvesting/ChoosingInvestments/MutualFunds/, accessed September 10, 2013

Haslem, J. A. (2010): Mutual Funds: Portfolio Structures, Analysis, Management, and Stewardship, Hoboken: John Wiley & Sons

Hereil, P. / Mitaine, P. / Moussavi, N. / Roncalli, T. (2010): Mutual Fund Ratings and Performance Persistence, Paris: Lyxor Asset Management, retrieved from http://www.thierry-roncalli.com/download/lwp-mfr.pdf, accessed February 6, 2013

HSBC (2005): Investmentfonds: Ein Leitfaden für ein besseres Verständnis der Fondswelt, Düsseldorf: HSBC Trinkaus Investment Products

ICI (2005): Supplementary Tables: Industry Statistic Q1/2005, Washington D.C.: Investment Company Institute, retrieved from http://www.ici.org/pdf/ww_03_05_sup_tables.pdf, accessed September 10, 2013

ICI a, (2013): Worldwide quarterly mutual fund market statistic, Washington D.C.: Investment Company Institute, retrieved from http://www.ici.org/research/stats/worldwide/data, accessed September 4, 2013

ICI b, (2013): Global market statistic Q1/2013, Washington D.C.: Investment Company Institute, retrieved from http://www.iciglobal.org/info/ww_03_13_sup_tables.xls, accessed September 5, 2013

ICI a, (n.a.): About ICI, Washington D.C.: Investment Company Institute, retrieved from http://www.ici.org/about_ici, accessed September 2, 2013

ICI b, (n.a.): Worldwide mutual fund data, Washington D.C.: Investment Company Institute, retrieved from http://www.ici.org/research/stats/worldwide/data, accessed September 2, 2013

IMCA (2003): The Handbook of Risk, Hoboken: John Wiley & Sons

Ippolito, R. A. (1992): Consumer Reaction to Measures of Poor Quality: Evidence from the Mutual Fund Industry, in: Journal of Law and Economics, vol. 35., pp. 45-70

Jensen, M. C. (1968): The Performance of Mutual Funds in the Period 1945-1964, in: Journal of Finance, vol. 23, no. 2, pp. 389-416., retrieved from http://www.e-m-h.org/Jens68.pdf, accessed October 7, 2013

Jones., C. P. (2009): Investments: Analysis and Management, 11th ed., Hoboken: John Wiley & Sons

Koch, P. C. (2007): Optimizing Distribution Systems in Asset Management, Hamburg: Helmut-Schmidt-Universität Hamburg

Latzko, D. A. (1998): Economies of scale in mutual fund administration, Pennsylvania: Pennsylvania State University

Lipper (2008): Lipper Global Classification – Extended, n.p.: Lipper, retrieved from http://www.lipperweb.com/docs/support/DataChange/Extended_LGC_Definitions.pdf, accessed September 20, 2013

Lipper (2013): About us, n.p.: Lipper, retrieved from http://www.lipperweb.com/AboutUs/Gateway.aspx, accessed September 18, 2013

Mayo, H. B. (2008): Investments: An Introduction, Mason: Thomson Higher Education

Mobius, M. (2007): Mutual Funds: An Introduction to the Core Concepts, Hoboken: John Wiley & Sons

Morningstar (2010): Looking at historical risk: Standard Deviation, retrieved from http://news.morningstar.com/classroom2/course.asp?docid=2927&page=2., accessed September 30, 2013

Morningstar (2013): Seid umschlungen, Neuemissionen!, in: Morningstar online, retrieved from http://www.morningstar.at/at/news/111255/seid-umschlungen-neuemissionen!.aspx, accessed November 7, 2013

Morningstar (n.a.): Morningstar Category, retrieved from http://www.morningstar.com/InvGlossary/morningstar_category.aspx, accessed September 20, 2013

Nofsinger, J. R. (2002): Investment Blunders of the Rich and Famous-- and what You Can Learn from Them, Upper Saddle River: Financial Times Prentice Hall

Pompian, M. (2012): Behavioral Finance and Investor Types: Managing Behavior to Make Better Investment Decisions, Hoboken: John Wiley & Sons

Reilly, F. K. (1994): Investment Analysis and Portfolio Management, 4th ed., Orlando: The Dryden Press

Reuters (2009): Funds fear ETF threat to active business, Monaco: Reuters, retrieved from http://www.reuters.com/article/2009/06/22/etf-fundforum-idUSLM37250720090622, accessed September 20, 2013

SEC a, (2007): Mutual Fund Investing: Look at More Than a Fund's Past Performance, New York City: U.S. Securities and Exchange Commission, retrieved from http://www.sec.gov/investor/pubs/mfperform.htm, accessed February 6, 2013

SEC b, (2007): Mutual Funds Without Active Management, New York City: U.S. Securities and Exchange Commission, retrieved from http://www.sec.gov/rss/ask_investor_ed/highcostmf.htm, accessed September 12, 2013

SEC (2010): Mutual Funds, Past Performance, New York City: U.S. Securities and Exchange Commission, retrieved from http://www.sec.gov/answers/mperf.htm, accessed February 6, 2013

SEC (2013): Guide to mutual funds, New York City, U.S. Securities and Exchange Commission, retrieved from http://www.sec.gov/investor/pubs/sec-guide-to-mutual-funds.pdf, accessed September 12, 2013

SEI (2013): Undertakings for Collective Investment in Transferable Securities (UCITS), n.p.: SEI Global Services: retrieved from http://www.seic.com/docs/IMS/SEI_UCITS_EU.pdf, accessed September 18, 2013

Sharpe, W. F. (1966): Mutual Fund Performance, in: Journal of Business, vol. 39, no. 1, pp. 119-138., retrieved from http://finance.martinsewell.com/fund-performance/Sharpe1966.pdf, accessed October 2, 2013

Siegel, A. (2011): Practical Business Statistics, Oxford: Academic Press

Sirri, E. R. / Tufano P. (1992): Flows, Performance, Fees and Services, Cambridge: Graduate School of Business Administration, Harvard University

Snelson, B. / Graham, M. (2008): Portfolio First Aid: Expert Advice for Healthier Investing, Mississauga: John Wiley & Sons Canada, Ltd.

Standard & Poor's (2013): Quantifying Investment Risk: The Sharpe Ratio, n.p.: Standard & Poor's, retrieved from http://fc.standardandpoors.com/sites/client/generic/axa/axa2/Article.vm?topic=5981&siteContent=8042, accessed October 2, 2013

Vanguard (2013): The mutual fund graveyard: An analysis of dead funds, Valley Forge: The Vanguard Group, Inc., retrieved from https://personal.vanguard.com/pdf/s362.pdf, accessed October 10, 2013

Yan, X. S. (2008): Liquidity, Investment Style, and the Relation between Fund Size and Fund Performance, in: Journal of Financial and Quantitative Analysis, vol 43, no.3, pp. 741-768, retrieved from http://business.missouri.edu/yanx/research/JFQA-433-07-Yan.pdf, accessed September 15, 2013 [illegible] S. (2008): [illegible] the Relation [illegible] Size and Firm Performance, in: Journal of Financial and Quantitative Analysis, [illegible] 2, [illegible] 63 [illegible]

Appendix A: correlation-test details: flow~percentage growth

Date:	08.2004	09.2004	10.2004	11.2004	12.2004	01.2005	02.2005	03.2005	04.2005	05.2005	06.2005	07.2005	08.2005	09.2005	10.2005	11.2005
Spearman's ρ	0.2421	0.2402	0.3257	0.3375	0.2913	0.2536	0.2434	0.2770	0.3681	0.3335	0.3200	0.3985	0.3685	0.2717	0.2910	0.2769
t-value	6.4046	6.6017	9.0670	9.5329	8.3878	7.2415	6.9811	8.2699	11.2328	10.0678	9.9233	12.5693	11.4696	8.3175	8.8719	8.4807
Significance¹	***	***	***	***	***	***	***	***	***	***	***	***	***	***	***	***
Significance²	***	***	***	***	***	***	***	***	***	***	***	***	***	***	***	***
Date:	12.2005	01.2006	02.2006	03.2006	04.2006	05.2006	06.2006	07.2006	08.2006	09.2006	10.2006	11.2006	12.2006	01.2007	02.2007	03.2007
Spearman's ρ	0.3176	0.3099	0.2979	0.2690	0.2941	0.2828	0.2640	0.3035	0.2759	0.3006	0.2492	0.2572	0.2149	0.1966	0.2117	0.2124
t-value	10.0157	9.7513	9.4866	8.4662	9.3686	9.0528	8.4101	9.7926	8.8385	9.7008	7.9423	8.2242	6.8227	6.2236	6.7623	6.8428
Significance¹	***	***	***	***	***	***	***	***	***	***	***	***	***	***	***	***
Significance²	***	***	***	***	***	***	***	***	***	***	***	***	***	***	***	***
Date:	04.2007	05.2007	06.2007	07.2007	08.2007	09.2007	10.2007	11.2007	12.2007	01.2008	02.2008	03.2008	04.2008	05.2008	06.2008	07.2008
Spearman's ρ	0.2040	0.2207	0.2360	0.2657	0.2758	0.2800	0.2444	0.2432	0.1924	0.1550	0.1430	0.0997	0.0623	0.1213	0.1448	0.1625
t-value	6.5212	7.1061	7.6793	8.7503	9.1516	9.2932	8.0627	8.0542	6.3632	5.1145	4.7337	3.3077	2.0660	4.0599	4.8542	5.4857
Significance¹	***	***	***	***	***	***	***	***	***	***	***	***	*	***	***	***
Significance²	***	***	***	***	***	***	***	***	***	***	***	***	*	***	***	***
Date:	08.2008	09.2008	10.2008	11.2008	12.2008	01.2009	02.2009	03.2009	04.2009	05.2009	06.2009	07.2009	08.2009	09.2009	10.2009	11.2009
Spearman's ρ	0.1965	0.2510	0.2270	0.2146	0.2165	0.1855	0.1609	0.1742	0.1354	0.1534	0.1365	0.1359	0.1506	0.1188	0.0804	0.0707
t-value	6.6576	8.6115	7.8029	7.3658	7.4764	6.4028	5.5570	6.0424	4.6470	5.2910	4.7181	4.7014	5.2596	4.1456	2.8051	2.4562
Significance¹	***	***	***	***	***	***	***	***	***	***	***	***	***	***	**	**
Significance²	***	***	***	***	***	***	***	***	***	***	***	***	***	***	**	*
Date:	12.2009	01.2010	02.2010	03.2010	04.2010	05.2010	06.2010	07.2010	08.2010	09.2010	10.2010	11.2010	12.2010	01.2011	02.2011	03.2011
Spearman's ρ	0.0530	0.0691	0.0789	0.0830	0.1462	0.1721	0.1902	0.1835	0.1882	0.1965	0.1506	0.1679	0.1344	0.1460	0.1240	0.1192
t-value	1.8304	2.4054	2.7454	2.8855	5.0905	6.0056	6.6319	6.4016	6.5523	6.8905	5.2258	5.8171	4.6089	5.0335	4.2699	4.1187
Significance¹	*	**	**	**	***	***	***	***	***	***	***	***	***	***	***	***
Significance²	o	*	**	**	***	***	***	***	***	***	***	***	***	***	***	***
Date:	04.2011	05.2011	06.2011	07.2011	08.2011	09.2011	10.2011	11.2011	12.2011	01.2012	02.2012	03.2012	04.2012	05.2012	06.2012	07.2012
Spearman's ρ	0.1751	0.1798	0.2049	0.2017	0.1942	0.1903	0.1685	0.1144	0.1258	0.1200	0.0774	0.1334	0.1402	0.0947	0.0560	0.1397
t-value	6.0843	6.2118	7.1625	7.0291	6.7407	6.6141	5.8085	3.9115	4.3026	4.1003	2.6178	4.5291	4.7759	3.1976	1.8733	4.7167
Significance¹	***	***	***	***	***	***	***	***	***	***	**	***	***	***	*	***
Significance²	***	***	***	***	***	***	***	***	***	***	**	***	***	**	o	***
Date:	08.2012	09.2012	10.2012	11.2012	12.2012	01.2013	02.2013	03.2013	04.2013	05.2013	06.2013	07.2013	08.2013			
Spearman's ρ	0.1688	0.1351	0.1641	0.1640	0.1508	0.1390	0.1546	0.1559	0.1372	0.1367	0.1159	0.1339	0.1513			
t-value	5.7252	4.5574	5.5529	5.5605	5.0814	4.6772	5.2013	5.2392	4.5939	4.5707	3.8572	4.4717	5.0527			
Significance¹	***	***	***	***	***	***	***	***	***	***	***	***	***			
Significance²	***	***	***	***	***	***	***	***	***	***	***	***	***			

Legend: ¹) Significance under a one-sided t-test, ²) Significance under a two-sided t-test; Significance codes: "***" 0.1% level, "**" 1% level, "*" 5% level., "o" 10% level.

Appendix B: correlation-test details: flow~volatility

Date:	08.2004	09.2004	10.2004	11.2004	12.2004	01.2005	02.2005	03.2005	04.2005	05.2005	06.2005	07.2005	08.2005	09.2005	10.2005	11.2005
Spearman's ρ	0.0351	-0.0434	-0.0097	-0.0093	-0.0229	0.0110	-0.0343	-0.0649	-0.0751	-0.0698	-0.0812	-0.0873	-0.1061	-0.0775	-0.0059	0.0098
t-value	0.9026	1.1584	0.2566	0.2474	0.6299	0.3028	0.9561	1.8670	2.1364	1.9901	2.3924	2.5351	3.0884	2.2889	0.1712	0.2894
Significance[1]								*	*	*	**	**	**	*		
Significance[2]								o	*	*	*	*	**	*		
Date:	**12.2005**	**01.2006**	**02.2006**	**03.2006**	**04.2006**	**05.2006**	**06.2006**	**07.2006**	**08.2006**	**09.2006**	**10.2006**	**11.2006**	**12.2006**	**01.2007**	**02.2007**	**03.2007**
Spearman's ρ	0.0575	0.0779	0.0739	0.1233	0.1266	0.1247	0.1429	0.1579	0.1603	0.1622	0.1634	0.1644	0.1490	0.1407	0.1335	0.1366
t-value	1.7228	2.3389	2.2534	3.7659	3.8856	3.8610	4.4373	4.9167	4.9990	5.0600	5.1136	5.1505	4.6723	4.4107	4.2066	4.3419
Significance[1]	*	**	*	***	***	***	***	***	***	***	***	***	***	***	***	***
Significance[2]	o	*	*	***	***	***	***	***	***	***	***	***	***	***	***	***
Date:	**04.2007**	**05.2007**	**06.2007**	**07.2007**	**08.2007**	**09.2007**	**10.2007**	**11.2007**	**12.2007**	**01.2008**	**02.2008**	**03.2008**	**04.2008**	**05.2008**	**06.2008**	**07.2008**
Spearman's ρ	0.0931	0.0500	0.0424	0.0511	0.0589	0.0648	0.0462	0.0427	0.0558	0.0712	0.0694	0.0921	0.1347	0.0859	-0.0135	-0.0328
t-value	2.9244	1.5733	1.3410	1.6254	1.8817	2.0686	1.4784	1.3744	1.8129	2.3257	2.2803	3.0538	4.4947	2.8635	0.4467	1.0945
Significance[1]	**	o	o	o	*	*	o	o	*	*	*	**	***	**		
Significance[2]	**				o	*			o	*	*	**	***	**		
Date:	**08.2008**	**09.2008**	**10.2008**	**11.2008**	**12.2008**	**01.2009**	**02.2009**	**03.2009**	**04.2009**	**05.2009**	**06.2009**	**07.2009**	**08.2009**	**09.2009**	**10.2009**	**11.2009**
Spearman's ρ	-0.0390	-0.0345	0.0237	-0.0430	-0.0187	-0.0031	0.0228	0.0094	-0.0054	0.0306	-0.0003	-0.0245	-0.0056	-0.0104	-0.0226	0.0005
t-value	1.2977	1.1463	0.7942	1.4439	0.6316	0.1054	0.7781	0.3205	0.1843	1.0422	0.0099	0.8385	0.1946	0.3608	0.7860	0.0190
Significance[1]	o			o												
Significance[2]																
Date:	**12.2009**	**01.2010**	**02.2010**	**03.2010**	**04.2010**	**05.2010**	**06.2010**	**07.2010**	**08.2010**	**09.2010**	**10.2010**	**11.2010**	**12.2010**	**01.2011**	**02.2011**	**03.2011**
Spearman's ρ	0.0240	0.0232	0.0067	0.0236	0.0641	0.0683	0.0636	0.0538	0.0474	0.0279	0.0299	0.0404	0.0237	-0.0006	0.0251	0.0130
t-value	0.8269	0.8059	0.2309	0.8182	2.2132	2.3541	2.1831	1.8483	1.6233	0.9584	1.0261	1.3798	0.8071	0.0215	0.8585	0.4458
Significance[1]					*	**	*	*	o			o				
Significance[2]					*	*	*	o								
Date:	**04.2011**	**05.2011**	**06.2011**	**07.2011**	**08.2011**	**09.2011**	**10.2011**	**11.2011**	**12.2011**	**01.2012**	**02.2012**	**03.2012**	**04.2012**	**05.2012**	**06.2012**	**07.2012**
Spearman's ρ	-0.0424	-0.0717	-0.0750	-0.0594	-0.0902	-0.0641	-0.0677	-0.0548	-0.0391	-0.0533	-0.0731	-0.0936	-0.1052	-0.0901	-0.0912	-0.0803
t-value	1.4524	2.4421	2.5726	2.0296	3.0849	2.1908	2.3037	1.8633	1.3279	1.8096	2.4700	3.1653	3.5677	3.0402	3.0583	2.6926
Significance[1]	o	**	**	*	**	*	*	*	o	*	**	***	***	**	**	**
Significance[2]		*	*	*	**	*	*	o		o	*	**	***	**	**	**
Date:	**08.2012**	**09.2012**	**10.2012**	**11.2012**	**12.2012**	**01.2013**	**02.2013**	**03.2013**	**04.2013**	**05.2013**	**06.2013**	**07.2013**	**08.2013**			
Spearman's ρ	-0.0821	-0.0701	-0.0345	-0.0283	0.0141	0.0177	0.0334	0.0454	0.0228	-0.0047	-0.0193	-0.0249	-0.0337			
t-value	2.7558	2.3492	1.1537	0.9484	0.4691	0.5896	1.1111	1.5089	0.7551	0.1563	0.6368	0.8237	1.1141			
Significance[1]	**	**						o								
Significance[2]	**	*														

Legend: [1]) Significance under a one-sided t-test, [2]) Significance under a two-sided t-test; Significance codes: "***" 0.1% level, "**" 1% level, "*" 5% level., "o" 10% level.

Appendix C: correlation-test details: flow~Sharpe ratio

Date:	08.2004	09.2004	10.2004	11.2004	12.2004	01.2005	02.2005	03.2005	04.2005	05.2005	06.2005	07.2005	08.2005	09.2005	10.2005	11.2005
Spearman's ρ	0.2375	0.2567	0.3269	0.3389	0.3168	0.2636	0.2442	0.3826	0.3970	0.3899	0.3792	0.4116	0.3719	0.2652	0.2660	0.2484
t-value	6.2754	7.0885	9.1066	9.5796	9.2007	7.5490	7.0049	11.8786	12.2736	12.0499	12.0380	13.0656	11.5917	8.1024	8.0483	7.5475
Significance¹	***	***	***	***	***	***	***	***	***	***	***	***	***	***	***	***
Significance²	***	***	***	***	***	***	***	***	***	***	***	***	***	***	***	***
Date:	**12.2005**	**01.2006**	**02.2006**	**03.2006**	**04.2006**	**05.2006**	**06.2006**	**07.2006**	**08.2006**	**09.2006**	**10.2006**	**11.2006**	**12.2006**	**01.2007**	**02.2007**	**03.2007**
Spearman's ρ	0.2890	0.2824	0.2637	0.2118	0.2576	0.2048	0.1643	0.1572	0.1207	0.1279	0.0892	0.0748	0.0487	0.0398	0.0753	0.0691
t-value	9.0274	8.8052	8.3083	6.5689	8.1176	6.4243	5.1183	4.8924	3.7440	3.9680	2.7648	2.3180	1.5111	1.2375	2.3568	2.1791
Significance¹	***	***	***	***	***	***	***	***	***	***	**	*	o		**	*
Significance²	***	***	***	***	***	***	***	***	***	***	**	*			*	*
Date:	**04.2007**	**05.2007**	**06.2007**	**07.2007**	**08.2007**	**09.2007**	**10.2007**	**11.2007**	**12.2007**	**01.2008**	**02.2008**	**03.2008**	**04.2008**	**05.2008**	**06.2008**	**07.2008**
Spearman's ρ	0.1118	0.2315	0.2390	0.2426	0.2189	0.2237	0.2220	0.2358	0.1696	0.1237	0.1271	0.0812	0.0261	0.0746	0.1709	0.1748
t-value	3.5203	7.4717	7.7823	7.9405	7.1545	7.3125	7.2828	7.7931	5.5831	4.0640	4.1987	2.6911	0.8645	2.4858	5.7514	5.9119
Significance¹	***	***	***	***	***	***	***	***	***	***	***	**		**	***	***
Significance²	***	***	***	***	***	***	***	***	***	***	***	**		*	***	***
Date:	**08.2008**	**09.2008**	**10.2008**	**11.2008**	**12.2008**	**01.2009**	**02.2009**	**03.2009**	**04.2009**	**05.2009**	**06.2009**	**07.2009**	**08.2009**	**09.2009**	**10.2009**	**11.2009**
Spearman's ρ	0.2066	0.2584	0.2266	0.2160	0.2186	0.1863	0.1655	0.1530	0.1119	0.1402	0.1226	0.1143	0.1466	0.1270	0.0710	0.0733
t-value	7.0116	8.8818	7.7893	7.4151	7.5545	6.4304	5.7219	5.2875	3.8314	4.8260	4.2297	3.9425	5.1159	4.4359	2.4757	2.5473
Significance¹	***	***	***	***	***	***	***	***	***	***	***	***	***	***	**	**
Significance²	***	***	***	***	***	***	***	***	***	***	***	***	***	***	*	*
Date:	**12.2009**	**01.2010**	**02.2010**	**03.2010**	**04.2010**	**05.2010**	**06.2010**	**07.2010**	**08.2010**	**09.2010**	**10.2010**	**11.2010**	**12.2010**	**01.2011**	**02.2011**	**03.2011**
Spearman's ρ	0.0635	0.0809	0.0764	0.1048	0.1912	0.2272	0.2297	0.2257	0.2250	0.2016	0.1395	0.1496	0.1271	0.1672	0.0979	0.1235
t-value	2.1937	2.8191	2.6582	3.6511	6.7096	8.0220	8.0792	7.9467	7.8938	7.0750	4.8333	5.1654	4.3558	5.7861	3.3617	4.2673
Significance¹	*	**	**	***	***	***	***	***	***	***	***	***	***	***	***	***
Significance²	*	**	**	***	***	***	***	***	***	***	***	***	***	***	***	***
Date:	**04.2011**	**05.2011**	**06.2011**	**07.2011**	**08.2011**	**09.2011**	**10.2011**	**11.2011**	**12.2011**	**01.2012**	**02.2012**	**03.2012**	**04.2012**	**05.2012**	**06.2012**	**07.2012**
Spearman's ρ	0.1806	0.1847	0.2161	0.2059	0.1973	0.1907	0.1750	0.1179	0.1288	0.1321	0.1205	0.1524	0.1682	0.1428	0.1136	0.1541
t-value	6.2823	6.3858	7.5740	7.1826	6.8512	6.6285	6.0380	4.0318	4.4070	4.5225	4.0903	5.1919	5.7563	4.8489	3.8171	5.2118
Significance¹	***	***	***	***	***	***	***	***	***	***	***	***	***	***	***	***
Significance²	***	***	***	***	***	***	***	***	***	***	***	***	***	***	***	***
Date:	**08.2012**	**09.2012**	**10.2012**	**11.2012**	**12.2012**	**01.2013**	**02.2013**	**03.2013**	**04.2013**	**05.2013**	**06.2013**	**07.2013**	**08.2013**			
Spearman's ρ	0.1726	0.1536	0.1810	0.1827	0.2074	0.1773	0.1849	0.1809	0.1608	0.1605	0.1303	0.1380	0.1515			
t-value	5.8580	5.1981	6.1434	6.2172	7.0597	6.0054	6.2554	6.1068	5.4049	5.3855	4.3450	4.6138	5.0618			
Significance¹	***	***	***	***	***	***	***	***	***	***	***	***	***			
Significance²	***	***	***	***	***	***	***	***	***	***	***	***	***			

Legend: ¹) Significance under a one-sided t-test, ²) Significance under a two-sided t-test; Significance codes: "***" 0.1% level, "**"1% level, "*" 5% level., "o" 10% level.

Appendix D: geographical database coverage: Lipper for Investment Management

LIPPER

LIPPER IM

DATABASE BREAKDOWN

ALL DATABASE SUBSCRIPTIONS INCLUDE ACCESS TO INDICES, CURRENCIES, MERGED AND LIQUIDATED FUNDS.

ALL REGION SUBSCRIPTIONS INCLUDE ACCESS TO INTERNATIONAL OFFSHORE AND HEDGE FUND DATA SETS.

REGION EUROPE

Austrian Mutual Funds (Reg. For Sale)	Polish Mutual Funds (Reg. For Sale)
French Mutual Funds (Reg. For Sale)	Portuguese Mutual Funds (Reg. For Sale)
German Mutual Funds (Reg. For Sale)	Belgian Mutual Funds (Reg. For Sale)
Italian Mutual Funds (Reg. For Sale)	Dutch Mutual Funds (Reg. For Sale)
Italian Pension Funds	Swedish Mutual Funds (Reg. For Sale)
Spanish Mutual Funds (Reg. For Sale)	Finnish Mutual Funds (Reg. For Sale)
Spanish Pension Funds	Norwegian Mutual Funds (Reg. For Sale)
Swiss Mutual Funds (Reg. For Sale)	Danish Mutual Funds (Reg. For Sale)
Swiss Pension Funds	Czech Mutual Funds (Reg. For Sale)
UK Mutual Funds (Reg. For Sale)	Slovak Mutual Funds (Reg. For Sale)
UK Pension and Insurance Funds	Lithuanian Mutual Funds (Reg. For Sale)
Latvian Mutual Funds (Reg. For Sale)	Estonian Mutual Funds (Reg. For Sale)
Hungarian Mutual Funds (Reg. For Sale)	

MIX
Papier aus verantwortungsvollen Quellen
Paper from responsible sources
FSC® C105338

If you have any concerns about our products,
you can contact us on
ProductSafety@springernature.com

In case Publisher is established outside the EU,
the EU authorized representative is:
Springer Nature Customer Service Center GmbH
Europaplatz 3, 69115 Heidelberg, Germany

Printed by Libri Plureos GmbH
in Hamburg, Germany